COLLINS COBUILD

ENGLISH GUIDES
10: DETERMINERS & QUANTIFIERS

Roger Berry

HarperCollins*Publishers*

HarperCollins Publishers
77-85 Fulham Palace Road
London W6 8JB

COBUILD is a trademark of William Collins Sons & Co Ltd

© HarperCollins Publishers Ltd 1997

First Published 1997

2 4 6 8 10 9 7 5 3 1

All rights reserved. No part of this book may be reproduced, stored
in a retrieval system, or transmitted in any form or by any means,
electronic, mechanical, photocopying, recording or otherwise,
without the prior permission in writing of the Publisher.

The author hereby asserts his moral rights to be identified as
the author of the work.

ISBN 0 00 375039 6

Corpus Acknowledgements

We would like to acknowledge the assistance of the many hundreds of
individuals and companies who have kindly given permission for
copyright material to be used in The Bank of English. The written
sources include many national and regional newspapers in Britain and
overseas; magazine and periodical publishers; and book publishers in
Britain, the United States, and Australia. Extensive spoken data has
been provided by radio and television broadcasting companies; research
workers at many universities and other institutions; and numerous
individual contributors. We are grateful to them all.

Computer typeset by Tradespools Ltd, Frome, Somerset.

Printed and bound in Great Britain by
Caledonian International Book Manufacturing Ltd, Glasgow, G64.

http://www.cobuild.collins.co.uk

Contents

Foreword   v

Chapter 1: Introduction   1
1.1 Determiners and quantifiers
1.2 What are determiners?
1.3 Definite and indefinite determiners
1.4 Determiners and articles
1.5 Type of noun
1.6 What are quantifiers?
1.7 Pronoun usage
1.8 Other features of determiners and quantifiers
1.9 Combinations of determiners
1.10 A summary of the properties of determiners

Chapter 2: Possessive determiners   20
2.1 Uses of possessive determiners
2.2 Meanings of possessive determiners
2.3 Possessive determiners with nouns indicating actions or events
2.4 Possessive determiners with **own**

Chapter 3: Demonstratives   31
3.1 Uses as determiners and pronouns
3.2 The difference in meaning between **this** and **that**, and **these** and **those**
3.3 Other ways of using **this** and **that**
3.4 Personal pronouns as demonstratives

Chapter 4: 'Wh'-word determiners   45
4.1 General uses of 'wh'-word determiners
4.2 In questions: **what, which, whose**
4.3 In relative clauses: **which, whose**
4.4 In noun clauses: **what, which, whose**
4.5 Uses of **whatever, whichever, whoever's**

Chapter 5: Numbers and similar determiners   55
5.1 Cardinal numbers: **one, two, three**, etc
5.2 Special uses of **one**
5.3 Ordinal numbers: **first, second, third**, etc
5.4 Multipliers: **twice, three times**, etc
5.5 Fractions: **a third, two-fifths**, etc
5.6 Uses of **half**

Chapter 6: Talking about the existence of an amount or number of something   73
6.1 Basic meaning of **some**
6.2 Other uses of **some**
6.3 Uses of **any**
6.4 Uses of **no**

Chapter 7: Talking about the whole of something   80

7.1 Major uses of **all**
7.2 Other ways of using **all**
7.3 Expressions with **all**
7.4 Comparison of **all** and **whole**
7.5 Uses of **every**
7.6 Comparison of **every** and **all**
7.7 Uses of **each**
7.8 Comparison of **each** and **every**
7.9 Uses of **any**

Chapter 8: Talking about a large amount or number of something   101

8.1 General uses of **much** and **many**
8.2 Uses of **much**
8.3 Uses of **many**
8.4 Adverb uses of **much**
8.5 Intensifiers with **much** and **many**
8.6 Expressions with **much**
8.7 Uses of **more** and **most**
8.8 Other ways of talking about a large amount or number of something

Chapter 9: Talking about a small amount or number of something   124

9.1 Basic uses of **little** and **a little**
9.2 Uses of **less** and **least**
9.3 Adverb uses of **little**, **a little**, **less**, and **least**
9.4 Uses of **few** and **a few**
9.5 Uses of **fewer** and **fewest**

Chapter 10: Talking about a group of two   137

10.1 Uses of **both**
10.2 Uses of **either**
10.3 Uses of **neither**

Chapter 11: Other determiners and quantifiers   143

11.1 Uses of **several**
11.2 Uses of **enough**
11.3 Uses of **such**
11.4 Uses of **what**
11.5 Uses of **rather** and **quite**

Exercises   154

Answer Key   177

Index   180

Foreword

The *Guide to Determiners and Quantifiers* is one of a series of COBUILD ENGLISH GUIDES to particular areas of difficulty for learners of English.

The author, Roger Berry, has taught English and Applied Linguistics to students in ten different countries on three continents. This is the second book he has written for COBUILD; his earlier *Guide to Articles* remains a cornerstone of this popular series.

Determiners and Quantifiers is, in a sense, a continuation or companion work to the earlier *Guide*. As the author makes clear in the opening chapter, the definite and indefinite articles can be considered as the two most important members of a much larger set of words, namely determiners. Determiners, in turn, are closely related to quantifiers, indeed are often the same words, distinguished only by the syntactic patterns in which they are used. It therefore makes sense to cover both word classes in the same volume, together with the associated uses of these words as pronouns and adverbs. Many idiomatic phrases containing these words are also included.

The terms 'determiner' and 'quantifier' are unfamiliar to most students of English, and even to many teachers, yet they cover some of the most frequently occurring words in the language. Indeed, the first four paragraphs of this Foreword contain no fewer than eighteen instances of determiners and quantifiers (not to mention the numerous occurrences of the definite and indefinite articles).

The book is organized along the following lines:

Chapter 1 deals with definitions and broad issues of principle, and seeks to classify individual determiners according to criteria of 'definiteness', the types of nouns they are used with, and the various combinations they can enter into.

Chapters 2 and 3 discuss the two major classes of 'definite' determiners, namely possessives ('my', 'your', etc) and demonstratives ('this', 'that', etc).

Chapter 4 looks at the 'wh'-determiners ('what', 'which', 'whose') and the ways they are used in questions and subordinate clauses.

Chapters 5 to 10 are concerned with a wide range of different determiners, as a glance at the Contents page will show, but what they all have in common is their 'quantifying' function. Within this category, there is a broad distinction to be made between those that imply a specific quantity (Chapters 5, 7, and 10), and those that imply an unspecified quantity (Chapters 6, 8, and 9). In these chapters can be found useful sections comparing and contrasting various pairs of closely related words, such as 'all' and 'every' (Chapter 7), 'some' and 'any' (Chapter 6), or 'much' and 'many' (Chapter 8), which can cause difficulty for learners of English and lead to mistakes.

Chapter 11 brings together various individual determiners, such as 'several', 'enough', and 'such', that do not clearly belong to any of the major categories previously discussed.

The author adopts a consistent approach throughout; for each determiner and quantifier, the meanings and syntactic patterns are first explained in simple, non-technical language, and then illustrated by means of real examples. Margin headings are included for ease of reference. Many of the most important points are taken up again at the end of the book, in a comprehensive and varied set of exercises which follow the order of the chapters, thus allowing students to systematically reinforce and revise what they have learned through studying the text. The Index will be of help in this respect.

This book, like all COBUILD books, is derived from studying the evidence in The Bank of English, a massive corpus of language now containing over 300 million words. The examples are taken directly from the corpus, and the frequency of words affects the prominence given to them here. The emphasis on real language ensures that the learner is able to observe how determiners and quantifiers are used by actual native speakers of English, and can then go on to use them, in a natural and convincing way, in his or her own writing and conversation.

We hope that you find this book helpful and easy to use. Please write to us with any comments or suggestions about how to improve COBUILD publications. We have set up an e-mail address (editors@cobuild.collins.co.uk) to make it easier for users to correspond with us. Alternatively, you can write to us at the following address:

COBUILD
Institute of Research and Development
University of Birmingham Research Park
Vincent Drive
Birmingham B15 2SQ

The COBUILD Series

Founding Editor-in-Chief John Sinclair

Publishing Director Gwyneth Fox

Editorial Team

Editor	John Williams		
Editorial Advice	Terry Shortall	*Editorial Assistance*	Alice Grandison Beth Szörényi
Computer Staff	Jeremy Clear Tim Lane	*Secretarial Staff*	Sue Crawley Michelle Devereux

Acknowledgements: The author would also like to thank Jane Bradbury, Gill Francis, Petek Kurtböke, Belén Labrador de la Cruz, and Dave Willis for their help at various stages in the production of this *Guide*.

To Mum and Dad

1 General Information

1.1 Determiners and quantifiers

This book is about some of the most important words in English: ***determiners*** and ***quantifiers***. Determiners and quantifiers are not two separate groups of words; most of the words in this book are both determiners and quantifiers, though some are only determiners. Whether a word is a determiner or quantifier depends on the pattern of words it is used in; these patterns are described separately below in 1.2 and 1.6. In addition, some of these words can also be pronouns or adverbs; these uses are dealt with in 1.7 and 1.8.

frequency Determiners are among the most frequent words in the English language. For example, in The Bank of English, the following determiners appear among the 200 most frequent words in English:

a, an	her	no	these
all	his	one	this
any	its	our	those
both	little	some	three
each	many	such	two
few	more	that	what
first	most	the	which
five	much	their	your
four	my		

In every sentence you are likely to find at least one determiner, so it is clear that these words are very important if you want to understand English, and speak or write it proficiently.

determiners with similar meanings One of the reasons why these words are so difficult is that their meanings in some cases are very similar; in many languages there is only one word where English has two. This book will help you with these difficult but important distinctions, for example:

1

Chapter 1

- the difference between pairs of words such as 'much' and 'many', 'few' and 'little'
- when to use 'some' or 'any'
- the difference between 'few' and 'a few', 'little' and 'a little'
- when to use 'all', 'every', or 'each'
- the difference between 'this' and 'that', 'these' and 'those'.

different uses and meanings

Another reason why these words are so difficult is that some of them have meanings and uses which have nothing to do with determiners and quantifiers. For example, 'little' can be an adjective as well; 'that' can be a relative pronoun; 'one' can be a personal pronoun. In this book you will find help in distinguishing these different uses.

1.2 What are determiners?

position in the noun group

Determiners have two important, related features. In terms of *structure*, they are the first part of a noun group; that is, they come before any of the other words that go with a noun.

About two hundred people gathered this afternoon outside the American embassy.

There are three noun groups in this sentence. All of them start with determiners of one kind or other: 'two hundred', 'this' and 'the'. In the last one there is an adjective between the determiner and the noun.

Sometimes there is no determiner with a noun.

Money was never important to him.
Your mother lives in China now.

In other cases there can be more than one determiner, up to a total of four (see **1.9**).

Putting all these feelings into words was not easy.

the meaning of determiners

In terms of *meaning*, they help to 'determine' the noun. That is, they relate the noun to the context in

Definite and indefinite determiners

which speech or writing takes place; they determine what a noun in one particular case is referring to. For example:

- They relate nouns to the speaker (or writer) and listener (or reader) in terms of nearness or distance ('this', 'that', 'these', 'those').

- They relate nouns to people through the idea of possession or some other close association ('my', 'your', 'their', etc).

- They identify a quantity of something, either in precise terms using a number or fraction, or in vague terms with words like 'some', 'many', or 'few'.

The reason why determiners come first in the noun group is that they carry information for the reader or listener which will help them to identify what the writer or speaker is talking about. These features are often fairly temporary or variable. For instance, 'this idea', in another situation or for another person, could be 'that idea'. Put another way, determiners are the words which allow people to reuse the same nouns endlessly for countless situations, to talk about countless different things. Proper nouns, which usually only refer to one thing, do not have determiners.

1.3 Definite and indefinite determiners

It is normal to distinguish two types of determiner: **definite** and **indefinite**. (In the *Collins COBUILD English Grammar* these were called **specific** and **general** determiners.)

definite determiners With **definite determiners**, such as 'the', demonstratives ('this', 'that', 'these', 'those') and possessives ('my', 'your', etc), the use of a determiner tells the listener or reader that they are already familiar with what you are talking about, that it is already established in their awareness.

Make sure the bread is quite cool.

Chapter 1

I don't like that idea much.
He shook his head gravely.

indefinite determiners With ***indefinite determiners***, there is no suggestion that the following noun is something familiar, or that it is established as a separate entity.

He filled a glass and drank it down.
Eric suddenly got an idea. 'Hey, let's have a pool party!' he said.
Many shops in the capital are closed.
There are few things I enjoy more than walking round an old cemetery.
First ask yourself some questions.

'which' and 'what' The concept of definiteness can explain the difference between 'what' and 'which' when they are used in questions; 'what' is indefinite, while 'which' is definite.

What colours did you see?
Which idea do you think is best?

'Which' tells readers and listeners that they should be familiar with the group of items mentioned; it is definite. 'What' does not. So if you say 'Which book do you want?', there is a probably a limited range of books to choose from, which your listener is aware of. If you say 'What book do you want?', the choice is relatively unlimited.

The borderline between definiteness and indefiniteness is not always clear. 'Both', for example, is usually grouped with indefinite determiners, but it undoubtedly has an idea of definiteness; it refers to something in the text or the environment that is familiar, or established in the mind of the reader or listener. That is why 'both' and 'both the' mean the same thing (see **10.1**).

1.4 Determiners and articles

The ***definite article*** 'the' and the ***indefinite article*** 'a' (and 'an') are also determiners. In the same way as all the other determiners, they come at the start of the

Determiners and articles

noun group and serve the same function of 'determining' the noun, that is, identifying it or relating it to its context.

Even that was an error.
The rug was stained.

But in one way they are unlike other determiners. This is the fact that they cannot be quantifiers or pronouns. You can say 'I like that car' and 'I like that'; but while you can say 'I like the car', you cannot say 'I like the'.

articles as basic determiners

One way to think of articles is to regard them as the basic determiners in terms of definiteness. That is, the definite article 'the' is the form to use when definiteness is indicated, but without the extra meanings of words like the possessives ('my', 'your', etc) or the demonstratives ('this', 'those', etc). In the same way, 'a' and 'an' are used to indicate indefiniteness when no other meaning is involved.

frequency of articles

Articles are even more common than the other determiners. 'The' is the most frequent word in English and 'a' (with 'an') is the fourth most frequent. For this reason, and for the fact that 'the' in particular has many different but related uses, it would be impossible to deal with them properly in such a book as this. You are advised to refer to *Collins COBUILD English Guides 3: Articles*, which is all about them.

zero article

In some books you will find mention of a *zero article* for cases where nouns have no article. Linguists have introduced this concept to allow them to say that all noun groups have a determiner of one kind or other; sometimes this is represented by nothing. This makes their accounts of English neater, but it can be confusing; in particular, it does not explain how some noun groups can have more than one determiner. This book does not talk about the zero article (or *zero determiner*), but in some cases it makes a clear comparison between sentences with a determiner such as 'some', and those with no determiner.

Chapter 1

1.5 Type of noun

The type of noun is very important for determiner usage; many determiners can only occur with certain types of noun. Basically, there are two factors which are important: whether a noun is count or uncount and, if it is count, whether it is singular or plural.

uncount nouns

Uncount nouns are nouns like 'sugar', 'bread', and 'honesty' which occur only in the singular and cannot be counted. That is, you cannot say 'a sugar', or 'two breads', or 'three honesties'. This usually applies to abstract concepts, and substances which are regarded as being impossible to divide up; this includes some words, such as 'furniture' and 'information', which in other languages can be counted.

He had only bread and soup for Sunday dinner.
I've just bought some new furniture.
He had neither charm nor humour.

You could not say 'breads', 'soups', 'furnitures', 'charms', or 'humours' here.

count nouns

Count nouns are those which can be counted and which can be used in both the singular and the plural. So you can say, for example, 'one dog', 'one pen', or 'one idea' and also 'two dogs', 'two pens', 'two ideas'.

I can't afford a car.
We want answers.
I have two younger brothers and one sister.

determiners grouped according to type of noun

Determiners can be put into a number of groups according to which types of noun they go with.

- Some determiners can go with all types of noun, for example 'my', 'your' (and other possessives), 'which', 'what', 'whose', as well as 'any', 'some' (depending on the particular use), and 'no'.

- Some determiners can go with plural count nouns and uncount nouns, but not with singular count nouns, for example 'all', 'enough', 'more', and 'most'.

What are quantifiers?

- Some determiners can go with singular count nouns and uncount nouns, but not with plural count nouns, for example 'this' and 'that'.

- Some determiners only go with singular count nouns, for example 'each', 'either', 'every', and 'neither'.

- Some determiners only go with plural count nouns, for example 'both', 'many', 'several', 'few', 'these', and 'those'.

- Some determiners only go with uncount nouns, for example 'much', 'little', 'a little', 'less', 'least'.

There are no determiners which can go with both singular and plural count nouns but not with uncount nouns.

You will find these possibilities and limitations described in full in each of the chapters. In addition there is a summary in the table on pages 18-19.

conversion of nouns

Sometimes it may seem there are exceptions to the rules given above; for example, it is possible to say 'She's all heart', where 'all' is being used with what seems to be a singular count noun ('one heart', 'two hearts'). In fact, in this case the word 'heart' has been changed, or converted, to an uncount noun; it is being used to denote a substance with the metaphorical meaning of 'kindness'.

One sister was all head, the other all heart.

1.6 What are quantifiers?

In some books the word ***quantifier*** means a group of words such as 'some', 'many', 'much', 'few', or 'little', which identify a quantity of something.

In this book the meaning of 'quantifier' is slightly different. It refers to words that can be used in a particular pattern, that is, when they are followed by 'of' and then a definite noun group.

Chapter 1

> *Many of the demonstrators came armed with iron bars and hammers.*
> *You can fool all of the people some of the time.*

definite noun groups
A ***definite noun group*** can begin with the definite article 'the' (as above), or with one of the other definite determiners described in **1.3** above, such as demonstratives or possessives.

> *Each of these types has a different penetrating power.*
> *Some of their language is explicit.*

Definite noun groups also include personal pronouns such as 'us' or 'them'.

> *I feel sorry for both of us.*
> *Some of them have been doing steady business ever since.*

In all of these cases the quantifier used is the same as an indefinite determiner and indicates a particular quantity of the following noun group. Words that are definite determiners cannot usually be quantifiers. You cannot say, for example, 'These of the people are tall'.

without 'of'
With some words such as 'both', 'all', and 'half', there is an alternative to the quantifier construction; you can leave out 'of' with no change of meaning.

> *He's about to lose both the women in his life.*
> *You need not worry about memorizing all these prepositions.*
> *It is taking more than half my time.*

Such words are sometimes called ***predeterminers*** (see **1.9** below). With most words, however, you cannot leave out 'of'; there is no alternative to the quantifier construction. For example, you cannot say 'Some their language is explicit'. (Of course, you can say 'Some language is explicit', but the meaning would be different).

The table on pages 18–19 shows which words can be quantifiers.

1.7 Pronoun usage

In addition to being determiners and quantifiers, most of the words in this book can also be **_pronouns_**. The table in **1.10** shows which can be pronouns. Of course, there are many other pronouns in the English language besides those covered here.

Pronouns are words which can take the place of noun groups. Which noun group is being referred to is made clear by the text, by the context of speech, or by general knowledge.

The hostages are very tired and have had no food. <u>Some</u> have been slightly injured.

In this case 'some' stands for 'some of the hostages', as the first sentence makes clear.

determiners which cannot be pronouns
The articles 'a', 'an', and 'the' cannot be pronouns. The same is true of 'no' and 'every'; you cannot say 'They have lots of money; we have no', or 'I liked them so much, I bought every'. 'No' has a pronoun equivalent: 'none' (see **6.4**). 'Every one' can sometimes be the pronoun equivalent of 'every' (see below).

possessive pronouns
The possessive determiners also have pronoun equivalents, except for 'his', which is both determiner and pronoun. The equivalents are shown in the table on pages 18–19.

formality
There may be restrictions on the use of some of these pronouns. Sometimes they may sound formal, as is the case with 'all' and 'much'.

<u>All</u> will be revealed.
<u>Much</u> depends on the weather.

compound pronouns
'Some', 'any', 'every', and 'no' form part of a number of compound pronouns. Compound pronouns ending in either '-one' or '-body' (with no difference in meaning) are used to refer to people. Compound pronouns ending in '-thing' refer to things.

Chapter 1

someone	anyone	everyone	no one
somebody	anybody	everybody	nobody
something	anything	everything	nothing

There is also a set of compound adverbs with '-where'.

| somewhere | anywhere | everywhere | nowhere |

The meanings of all of these compounds are related to the meanings of 'some', 'any', 'every', and 'no' when these words are used on their own. For example, 'everybody' means the same as 'every person', and 'anywhere' means 'in any place'.

Sometimes, instead of using a pronoun, you can use a determiner followed by 'one', for example 'each one'.

alternatives with 'one'

Each one has to be looked at on its own merits.

These alternatives with 'one' do not mean the same as the compound pronouns mentioned above. For example, 'every one' is not the same as 'everyone'. (However, note that the pronoun 'no one' is usually written as two words.) Further information can be found in the relevant sections.

1.8 Other features of determiners and quantifiers

adverb usage

Several of the words discussed in this book can also be adverbs, when they modify verbs, adjectives, or other adverbs. Their meaning is similar to the one they have when they are determiners or quantifiers.

Will it always be this hot?
I can't believe he was that good an actor.
Landlords say they will not wait any longer.
My back feels all achy
It didn't hurt much.
Grapes may be more acceptable.
That was the most important thing.
Lili opened her eyes a little wider.
If you feel confident you will be less anxious.

Other features of determiners and quantifiers

This offers the <u>least</u> painful compromise for the human race.
You've come to my rescue often <u>enough</u>.
He is <u>quite</u> interested in politics.
The reality was <u>rather</u> different.

With some of these, such as 'more', 'less', 'quite', and 'rather', the adverb use is in fact the most common. The table on pages 18–19 shows all the words which can have adverbial uses. These uses are then described further in the relevant sections.

delayed determiners Three words – 'all', 'both', and 'each' – can appear in unusual positions in the sentence, where they are separated from the noun group.

We'd <u>all</u> like to make easy money.
Liver and eggs are <u>both</u> good sources of natural iron.
The sergeants <u>each</u> carried one.

In these examples, 'all' refers to 'we', 'both' refers to 'liver and eggs', and 'each' to 'the sergeants'. More information about this use can be found in the relevant sections.

non-assertive contexts Certain determiners can only be used in what are called ***non-assertive contexts***. These are contexts such as negative sentences where the existence of what is being talked about is not being claimed, or 'asserted'. This affects 'any', 'much', and, to some extent, 'many'. So the affirmative counterparts of these sentences would be impossible in English.

I can't see <u>any</u> reason for this.
She has <u>never</u> needed <u>much</u> sleep.

Other non-assertive contexts include questions, conditionals, and after words that have a negative idea, such as 'few', 'little', 'hardly', 'only', 'seldom', 'without', 'fail', or 'prevent'.

Did it play <u>any</u> role at all in the presidential campaign?
Go slowly to see if there are <u>any</u> places where it is sticking.

Chapter 1

> *Very few all-girl bands have had <u>much</u> success in Australia.*
> *In recent years it has hardly been the source of <u>much</u> national pride.*
> *Then he moved forward without fear, without <u>any</u> emotion.*
> *The leadership's moderate stance has failed to win it <u>any</u> political benefits.*

'Much' can be used in assertive contexts, but then its use is formal.

> *The square was the scene of <u>much</u> fighting.*

In the same situation 'many' is also considered by some to be rather formal.

> *They have got <u>many</u> things in common.*

As well as these determiners and quantifiers, there are other words and expressions in English which, in some meanings, are limited to non-assertive contexts, for example 'yet', 'ever', and 'at all'.

formality Formality is also an important factor in determiner usage. The formality of 'much' and 'many' in assertive contexts has just been mentioned, as has that of 'much' and 'all' as pronouns (see **1.7**). Basically, the level of formality is determined by the situation in which language is being used. In formal situations, such as serious writing and some speaking (for example, official speeches), people plan much more and pay more attention to notions of correctness. In informal situations this is not the case.

The use of 'less' with plural count nouns instead of 'fewer' is regarded by some as informal, and by others as unacceptable (see **9.2**).

> *I did expect more food and <u>less</u> people.*

There are also many quantifying expressions such as 'a lot of' and 'plenty of', which are informal to some degree (see **8.8**).

> *There is <u>plenty of</u> the stuff about.*

modifying determiners

It is very common to modify determiners with adverbs.

The side effects made her sleep <u>nearly all</u> the time.
There are <u>very few</u> films of this sort.
I had <u>hardly any</u> strength left.

Common modifications of determiners are described in the relevant sections.

1.9 Combinations of determiners

It is possible to have more than one determiner in a noun group. There are a number of possible combinations of two determiners; these are dealt with in the various chapters. There are also a few possible combinations with three determiners, for example 'all the many possibilities'. In fact, it is theoretically possible to put four determiners together, for example 'all the many such possibilities'.

It is usual to explain the ordering of two or three determiners in terms of three possible positions which determiners can occupy. (There are a number of problems with this approach, which are dealt with below.)

central determiners

Words that can come in the middle position are sometimes called ***central determiners***. These include the most common determiners: the articles, the demonstratives, and the possessives.

They took him with them to all <u>the</u> many addresses.
If even half <u>these</u> 24 MPs are declared bankrupt the Government could lose its majority.
He kept the highest standards in all <u>his</u> many roles.

predeterminers in front of 'the'

The words that can occur before central determiners are sometimes called ***predeterminers***. The following words can come immediately in front of 'the' or other definite determiners: 'all', 'both', 'half', and multipliers ('twice', 'three times', etc).

<u>Both</u> his parents are still alive.
<u>All the</u> ironing is done.

Chapter 1

*Half the building was in flames.
And of course you get twice the profit.*

Other fractions ('one third', 'two-fifths', etc) are very rare as predeterminers. You can say 'one third the amount' but not 'one third the building'. (See **5.5** for further information about this.)

predeterminers in front of 'a'

A number of predeterminers can be used in front of the indefinite article and a singular count noun: 'half', 'such', 'many', 'what' (in exclamations), 'rather', and 'quite'.

*I ordered half a pint of lager.
Mother made such a fuss about it.
There could be many a slip before his ultimate end was achieved.
What a mess we have made of everything!
It was rather a pity.
He makes quite a noise.*

'Many a', 'such a', and 'what a' can all be treated as special cases to some extent. Both 'many' and 'such' also appear frequently after other determiners, and 'what' has other uses as a determiner where it does not occur before the indefinite article. In addition, 'many a' is unusual in combining singular and plural; and though it has a plural idea, it goes with a singular verb (see **8.3**).

postdeterminers

The words that can come after central determiners are sometimes called ***postdeterminers***. These include 'many', 'few', 'little', 'several', 'every', and numbers.

*No one can be blamed for the many errors of fact.
The few survivors staggered bleeding back into camp.
So why do his words carry such little weight?
I need to sell these four boxes of fruit.*

words which cannot combine with other determiners

Some words are never or rarely combined with other determiners. These include 'either', 'neither', 'each', and 'enough'. You cannot say, for example, 'I like these neither ideas'. Instead, you can sometimes use the quantifier construction with 'of'.

Combinations of determiners

Neither of these ideas has yet been put into action.

Sometimes there are two possible constructions: one with a quantifier, and one with a combination of determiners: 'many of the people' and 'the many people'. However, the meanings are different: 'many of the people' refers to a large quantity ('many') of a definite group of people; 'the many people' refers to a definite group of people which happens to be large.

determiners which can have different positions

There are a number of problems for this three-position approach to determiner ordering, because some words can have different positions.

- 'Every' can be placed before 'few' but also after possessives (with a difference in meaning).

Every few days there seemed to be another setback.
Television cameras would be monitoring his every step.

- 'Such' can be placed after a postdeterminer such as 'many', but can be a predeterminer before the indefinite article.

Is this the last of many such occasions?
Mother made such a fuss about it.

- 'Many' can be a either a predeterminer before the indefinite article, or a postdeterminer after definite determiners.

Many a successful store has paid its rent cheerfully.
None of her many lovers seemed to want to marry her.

These cases are all described in the relevant sections.

'a few' and 'a little'

'A few' and 'a little' are not regarded as combinations of two determiners but as single determiners. This is because both are used with types of nouns (plural and uncount) which cannot normally go with the indefinite article 'a'.

Chapter 1

common combinations of two determiners

Here are some common combinations of two determiners:

half **many** **such** **what** **rather** **quite**	in front of	**a, an**
my **your** **his** and other possessives	in front of	**every**
the possessives demonstratives	in front of	numbers **many** **little** **few** **several**
some **no** **all** **many** **few** **several**	in front of	**such**
fractions (including **half**) multipliers **all** **both**	in front of	**the** possessives demonstratives
all	in front of	**you** **them** (non-standard)

A summary of the properties of determiners

other combinations These other combinations are also possible:

some more	much more
some few	much less
any more	many more
any less	many fewer
any fewer	rather few
no more	quite few
no less	quite a few
no fewer	

More information about all these combinations will be found in the relevant sections.

1.10 A summary of the properties of determiners

The table on pages 18-19 summarizes the most important features of determiners. The first three columns show, for each word, whether it can be used as a quantifier, pronoun, or adverb. All the words in the table are determiners, so there is no separate column for this. The next three columns show whether the word can be used with the singular or plural of count nouns, or with uncount nouns. A tick (✓) indicates that the word can be used in the way shown; a cross (✗) that it cannot. The final column tells you where you will find a detailed discussion of the word in this *Guide*.

Groups of words such as numbers, fractions, and multipliers, which have an unlimited membership, are not included in the table. 'Own', and compound determiners such as 'whatever' and 'whichever', are also not included.

Chapter 1

TABLE SHOWING PROPERTIES OF DETERMINERS

The rows in the table marked as **any**[a] and **any**[b] represent the two distinct meanings of the word. Similarly, **what**[b] refers to the use of *what* in exclamations, and **what**[a] refers to its other uses.

	QUANTIFIER	PRONOUN	ADVERB	COUNT SING.	COUNT PL.	UNCOUNT	SECTION
all	✓	✓	✓	✗[1]	✓	✓	7.1–7.4
any[a]	✓	✓	✗	✗	✓	✓	6.3
any[b]	✓	✓	✗	✓	✓	✓	7.9
both	✓	✓	✗	✗	✓	✗	10.1
each	✓	✓	✗	✓	✗	✗	7.7, 7.8
either	✓	✓	✗	✓	✗	✗	10.2
enough	✓	✓	✓[2]	✗	✓	✓	11.2
every	✗	✗	✗	✓	✗	✗	7.5, 7.6
a few	✓	✓	✗	✗	✓	✗	9.4
few	✓	✓	✗	✗	✓	✗	9.4
fewer	✓	✓	✗	✗	✓	✗	9.5
fewest	✓	✓	✗	✗	✓	✗	9.5
her	✗	hers	✗	✓	✓	✓	2.1–2.3
his	✗	✓	✗	✓	✓	✓	2.1–2.3
its	✗	✓[3]	✗	✓	✓	✓	2.1–2.3
least	✓	✓	✓	✗	✗[4]	✓	9.2, 9.3
less	✓	✓	✓	✗	✗[4]	✓	9.2, 9.3
a little	✓	✓	✓	✗	✗	✓	9.1, 9.3
little	✓	✓	✓	✗	✗	✓	9.1, 9.3
many	✓	✓	✗	✗	✓	✗	8.1, 8.3, 8.5
more	✓	✓	✓	✗	✓	✓	8.7
most	✓	✓	✓	✗	✓	✓	8.7
much	✓	✓	✗	✗	✗	✓	8.1, 8.2, 8.4, 8.5
my	✗	mine	✗	✓	✓	✓	2.1–2.3
neither	✓	✓	✗	✓	✗	✗	10.3
no	✗[5]	✗[5]	✗	✓	✓	✓	6.4
our	✗	ours	✗	✓	✓	✓	2.1–2.3
quite	✗	✗	✓	✓[6]	✗	✗	11.5
rather	✗	✗	✓	✓[6]	✗	✗	11.5
several	✓	✓	✗	✗	✓	✗	11.1

A summary of the properties of determiners

	QUANTIFIER	PRONOUN	ADVERB	COUNT SING.	COUNT PL.	UNCOUNT	SECTION
some	✓	✓	✗	✗[7]	✓	✓	6.1, 6.2
such	✗	✗	✗	✓[6]	✓	✓	11.3
that	✗	✓	✓	✓	✗	✓	3.1–3.3
their	✗	theirs	✗	✓	✓	✓	2.1–2.3
these	✗	✓	✗	✗	✓	✗	3.1–3.3
this	✗	✓	✓	✓	✗	✓	3.1–3.3
those	✗	✓	✗	✗	✓	✗	3.1–3.3
us	✗	✓	✗	✗	✓	✗	3.4
we	✗	✓	✗	✗	✓	✗	3.4
what[a]	✗	✓	✗	✓	✓	✓	4.1–4.4
what[b]	✗	✗	✗	✓[6]	✓	✓	11.4
which	✓	✓	✗	✓	✓	✓	4.1–4.4
whose	✗	✓	✗	✓	✓	✓	4.1–4.4
you	✗	✓	✗	✗	✓	✗	3.4
your	✗	yours	✗	✓	✓	✓	3.4

Notes

1 'All' can be used with the singular of some count nouns.
2 As an adverb, 'enough' comes after the adjective or adverb it modifies.
3 As a pronoun, 'its' is very rare.
4 For some people it is acceptable to use 'less' and 'least' with the plural of count nouns.
5 'None' is in some ways the quantifier and pronoun equivalent of 'no'.
6 When used with the singular of a count noun, 'quite', 'rather', 'such', and 'what' (in this meaning) must be followed by 'a' or 'an'.
7 There are some less common uses of 'some' where it can go with the singular of count nouns (see Chapter 6).

2 Possessive determiners

my, your, his, her, its, our, their

my own, your own, his own, etc

One of the most obvious ways to identify or 'determine' nouns is to relate them to people, and that is what these words do. They are often called 'possessive adjectives' but in fact they are not adjectives but determiners.

In fact, the idea of possession is much too restricted for these words; they cover a whole range of different relationships between people and nouns which are described in **2.2** and **2.3** below.

For example 'your book' could mean the one that belongs to you, the one you wrote, the copy that the teacher lent you, and so on. 'Your horse' could be the one you own, the one you are riding, or the one you bet some money on. And in many cases the idea of possession does not apply at all, for example, 'your father', 'your chances', 'your boss'. There are also noun groups which indicate some action that the person has caused or experienced, or some state involving that person: 'my victory', 'her arrival', 'his dismissal', 'their absence'.

When you use a possessive determiner, you are telling your listener or reader that, because you have mentioned the 'possessor', they can identify what you are referring to.

A moment later there was a knock at <u>my door</u>.
The reports ought to be on <u>your desk</u> by now.
He paused, and shook <u>his head</u> gravely.
The Duchess hurled down <u>her pen</u>.
The word has found <u>its way</u> into the dictionaries.
He treats <u>our living room</u> as if it's a pig sty.
I walked down the street where I thought <u>their house</u> should be.

Uses of possessive determiners

The possessive determiners in these sentences tell the listener or reader *which* door, desk, head, pen, way, living room, or house you are talking about. The person you are referring to can be identified either from the general context, or because they have been mentioned in the text (e.g. 'the Duchess'). In the last example it is understood that 'their' refers to some people who have been mentioned before.

These words are dealt with in the following sections:

2.1 Uses of possessive determiners
2.2 Meanings of possessive determiners
2.3 Possessive determiners with nouns indicating actions or events
2.4 Possessive determiners with **own**

2.1 Uses of possessive determiners

My relates a noun group to the speaker (or writer), **our** to the speaker and someone else. **Your** relates a noun group to the listener (or reader) or to a number of listeners. **His**, **her**, **its** (singular), and **their** (plural) relate noun groups to people who are neither speakers nor listeners but who can be identified in some way.

relationship to personal pronouns

These seven words are related to personal pronouns in the following way.

	SUBJECT PERSONAL PRONOUN	OBJECT PERSONAL PRONOUN	**POSSESSIVE DETERMINER**	POSSESSIVE PRONOUN
FIRST PERSON SINGULAR	I	me	**my**	mine
SECOND PERSON	you	you	**your**	yours
THIRD PERSON SINGULAR MALE	he	him	**his**	his
THIRD PERSON SINGULAR FEMALE	she	her	**her**	hers
THIRD PERSON SINGULAR NON-HUMAN	it	it	**its**	—
FIRST PERSON PLURAL	we	us	**our**	ours
THIRD PERSON PLURAL	they	them	**their**	theirs

Chapter 2

The last column shows possessive pronouns, which are discussed below.

Remember that 'its' has no apostrophe ('). If there is an apostrophe ("it's") it is a short way of writing 'it is' or 'it has'. This can be quite difficult to remember and in fact a lot of native speakers find it confusing.

no changes in form
Possessive determiners have the same form whether the noun group is singular or plural, and count or uncount. There are no changes in form as in some languages.

I went back into my bedroom.
I was dancing with both children in my arms.
It urged the government to follow my advice.

not as pronouns
Unlike most determiners, you cannot use possessive determiners as pronouns, except in the case of 'his', where the determiner and pronoun are the same. In other cases there are different words, shown in the last column in the table above: 'mine', 'yours', 'hers', 'ours', and 'theirs'.

They were in the room next to mine.
Everything I have is yours.
He looked up and saw which window was his.
Is it his money or hers?
All your neighbours are noisier than ours.
But the risk is not theirs.

To use 'its' as a possessive pronoun is very unusual; sentences like 'The dog starts eating our food when its is finished' are extremely rare.

WARNING
Possessive determiners are already definite and so you cannot use them with 'a' (because it would be a contradiction) or with 'the' (because it would be unnecessary). You cannot say 'a my friend' or 'the my friend'. However, if you want to give an indefinite idea, you can say 'a friend of mine'; the plural would be 'friends of mine' or 'some friends of mine'.

She called in a friend of hers.
I saw a cousin of yours yesterday.

Uses of possessive determiners

Some friends of ours had a cottage at Boggle Hole.

If you say, for example, 'her friend', there is only one possible friend in question; 'a friend of hers' means one out of several possible friends.

'me' or 'my' before '-ing' There is still some argument about what form to use before the '-ing'-forms of verbs when they are used as nouns (sometimes referred to as *gerunds*). Both possessive determiners and object personal pronouns are used.

He doesn't mind my hanging round the kitchen.
Do you mind me talking to you like this?

For some people the use of 'me' is incorrect; for others 'my' is very formal.

after 'all', 'both', 'half' Possessive determiners can come after 'all', 'both', and 'half'.

All my other patients are fine.
He rested both his hands on the back of the chair.
Over half our sugar intake comes from snack foods.

Alternatives with 'of' are also possible: 'all of my other patients', 'both of his hands', 'half of our sugar intake'. There is no change in meaning.

'thy' There is one other possessive determiner, **thy**, but this is archaic, and is only found in very old texts (such as the Bible) or in those trying to appear very old. It is used for the second person singular.

Let not an enemy be thy neighbour.

genitive 's There is one more form which behaves very much like possessive determiners. This is **genitive 's**, which is used with noun groups to give the same idea of 'possession'.

Mother's cooking was horrible.
And that is just the start of John Major's troubles.
Keegan is the man in the street's choice as England manager.

They were led up to the altar to view the cathedral's treasures.

Such forms can also be used without following nouns.

The handbag was her mother's.

2.2 Meanings of possessive determiners

When possessive determiners are used with nouns they cover a wide range of relationships between the noun and the person involved. Some of these are described below.

- Objects in someone's possession or ownership

By using a possessive determiner you can suggest that the person is the owner of the thing involved.

Even the cost of getting your car back to your home is covered.
He'd also taken his CDs, his CD player, and his radio.
What's your dog called?

- Body parts

You use possessive determiners with parts of the body to relate them to the person involved.

I might even break your arm.

The sun was shining right into our eyes.

They are normally necessary even when the possessor is mentioned.

She shook her head.
She could see him sprawled flat on his back.

In the first example here, 'She shook the head' would refer to another head, not hers.

body parts with 'the' There are some cases, however, where the definite article is used when you might expect a possessive determiner.

Meanings of possessive determiners

The Duchess patted her on <u>the head</u>.
He took her by <u>the hand</u> and led her into the next room.
A youth was paralysed after being shot in <u>the neck</u>.
He said he'd got a pain in <u>the chest</u>.

This normally happens when there is also a preposition ('on', 'by', or 'in') in front, which shows that the body part is a location. This is not possible when the body part is affected as a whole; you could not say 'I broke her on the arm'. Also, it must be clear who the 'possessor' is (for example, 'her', 'a youth', and 'he' in the examples above). It would be unnecessary, repetitive even, to say 'patted her on her head', 'took her by her hand', and so on. What is possible, though, is to say 'patted her head' or 'took her hand'.

Sometimes, however, you can use a possessive determiner in this situation.

I feel a pain in <u>my neck</u> whenever I lift heavy objects.

'I feel a pain in the neck' is also possible.

Collins COBUILD English Guides 3: Articles deals with this in more detail.

- Personal relationships

With nouns referring to personal relationships, including family members, you use a possessive determiner to mention the person who is related.

I have done nothing to hurt <u>your brother</u>.
<u>Our boss</u> is a fresh air fanatic.
<u>Your doctor</u> may be able to help.

- Personal attributes

You can relate personal attributes such as age, height, and weight to a person by using a possessive determiner.

It's not a question of <u>your age</u>.
He was sensitive about <u>his height</u>.
What do they think of <u>your accent</u> in Scotland?

Chapter 2

- Personal feelings and thoughts

You can relate feelings and thoughts to the person who has them by using a possessive determiner.

The car crash shattered <u>her hopes</u> of competing at the Olympic Games.
Too many people blame <u>their failings</u> and <u>their unhappiness</u> on luck.
Scientists have taken a great interest in <u>his ideas</u>.

- Personal involvement

This category includes a whole range of possibilities where a person is involved with something in a general way.

Punters come up and ask 'How did <u>my horse</u> do?'
Tell them how <u>your day</u> has been.
You cannot go into <u>our classroom</u>.
She knew the reality that was <u>her London</u>.

The last example above could refer to her experience or perception of London, or to the parts of London she knew well.

2.3 Possessive determiners with nouns indicating actions or events

Sometimes the noun following a possessive determiner can be related to a verb which indicates an action or event. For instance, if you talk about 'his arrival' you imply that he arrived, is arriving, or will arrive. Presenting an action as a noun group allows you to talk about it easily, for example making it possible to thank someone for it.

Thank you for <u>your call</u>.

There are a number of grammatical relationships which can be expressed in this way; the two most obvious are where the person indicated by the possessive determiner would be the subject or object of the verb.

Possessives with nouns indicating actions or events

- Subject

Here the person would be the subject of the verb.

She sent a telegram announcing her arrival.
I thank you for your cooperation.
Our struggle is hard but our victory is certain.
Liu Bang ruled the state of Han and after his defeat of Xiang Yu, established the Han dynasty.

The person referred to with the possessive determiner does something: calls, arrives, cooperates, struggles, wins, or defeats. (Note that 'defeat' can also be an object noun, as in the first example below, but the following preposition is 'by', not 'of'.)

- Object

Here the person would be the object of the verb.

He blamed his back for his defeat by Carl Lewis.
They congratulated her on her election.
If you ever strike me, it will mean more than your dismissal.
Then at last I got my promotion to district inspector.

The person referred to with the possessive determiner has something done to them: someone defeats, elects, dismisses, or promotes them. If it is necessary to show the subject of the action, this can be done with a noun group starting with 'by', as in the first example above. This is similar to a passive ('He was defeated by Carl Lewis').

- Other events and states

Other events and states involving people can be mentioned quickly in a sentence by using a possessive determiner. In these cases the nouns may be derived from adjectives.

There was no cure for her illness.
We have been entertaining each other in your absence.

Here the person was ill or absent.

2.4 Possessive determiners with **own**

for emphasis You can put **own** after all the possessive determiners (or after genitive **'s**) in order to emphasize them.

I can find my own way out.
You make your own luck in this life.
She had her own secret to keep.
It did have its own balcony.
We'll have lunch in our own apartment.
Rachel and Chris had taken their own picnic lunch.
They were Sir George's own original curtains.

Sometimes 'own' emphasizes that a 'possession' is not shared.

I hope to get my own computer soon.
He will be given his own room where he can study privately.

If you want to emphasize 'own' itself you can put 'very' in front of it.

It will be your very own cat.

for contrast One particular kind of emphasis is when you want to contrast or compare one 'possessor' with another. You can also use 'own' in this case.

A few days after my own arrival, Miss Lewis joined us.

Here the contrast is with Miss Lewis's arrival, although it is not specifically mentioned. Sometimes the person being compared is not mentioned.

He thought of his own flat and how peaceful it was there.
As he did so, his own sense of guilt returned.

In these examples the contrast is with another person's flat (which he is probably standing in) or another person's sense of guilt. In other cases the other person can be identified with another possessive.

I accepted that my own well-being was joined to his.

Here 'his' means 'his well-being'.

Possessive determiners with 'own'

to distinguish possessors
Sometimes you can use 'own' to show who the 'possessor' is when there is more than one possibility; it picks out the subject of the sentence.

Mark slipped him his own passport.

This makes it clear that the passport is Mark's.

In all of these examples it would be possible in speech to leave out 'own' and stress the possessive determiner.

without a noun
You can use 'own' without a following noun.

She hurried out of the room and along the passage to her own.

not with other determiners
'Own' must be used with a possessive determiner (or genitive **'s**); you cannot use it with other determiners. So you cannot say 'an own room'. But if you want to give an idea of indefiniteness you can say 'a room of my own' or 'a room of her own'.

One day I would have a child of my own.
Mr Heseltine obviously had ideas of his own.
There may be a local cycling group you could join, or you might like to set up one of your own.

in expressions
If you do something **on** your **own**, you do it alone or without any help.

I enjoy being on my own rather than in a relationship.
Did Charley do all of it on his own?

If you **hold** your **own** in a situation or activity, you are as strong or as good as anyone else involved.

She could hold her own in any drinking session.

If you **make** something your **own**, you make it personal in some way.

Michael Goldfarb reports on John Major's battle to make the Conservative Party his own.
They take the technology, make it their own, and modify it to suit their own purposes.

Chapter 2

'own' as a verb 'Own' is used in one other important way: as a verb, with the meaning 'possess'.

She used to <u>own</u> all the property round here.

It is possible to have both uses of 'own' in the same sentence.

One day you could <u>own</u> your <u>own</u> factory.

3 Demonstratives

this, that, these, those

we, us, you

'This', 'that', 'these', and 'those' are called *demonstrative adjectives* or simply *demonstratives* (because in fact they are not adjectives). They help a speaker or writer to point to, or demonstrate, something that is in their environment. If it is regarded as 'close', **this** (singular) and **these** (plural) are used; if it is 'distant', **that** (singular) and **those** (plural) are used. These ideas of closeness and distance are not just a question of space, as **3.2** explains.

My family's lived in this area for generations.
These books may be appreciated better by older children.
I don't like that idea much.
There will be a perfectly logical explanation for all those deaths.

In certain situations, as **3.1** shows, 'that' and 'those' do not have any demonstrative idea.

These words are dealt with in the following sections:

    3.1 Uses as determiners and pronouns
    3.2 The difference in meaning between **this** and **that**, and **these** and **those**
    3.3 Other ways of using **this** and **that**
    3.4 Personal pronouns as demonstratives

Section **3.2** also discusses some other words that are used in a demonstrative-like way: **yon**, **yonder**, and **them**. For more information on another word which has a demonstrative idea, **such**, see **11.3**.

Section **3.4** deals with a rather special use of the personal pronouns **we**, **us**, and **you** as demonstratives.

Chapter 3

3.1 Uses as determiners and pronouns

Like all the words in this book, **this**, **that**, **these**, and **those** are closely related to nouns. They are either used with them, at the beginning of a noun group, that is, as determiners, or they are used on their own as noun groups, that is, as pronouns.

as determiners When they are determiners, 'this' and 'that' are used in singular noun groups, both count and uncount; 'these' and 'those' are used in plural noun groups.

Whoever had come up with this idea deserved a medal.
But what happens when all this money is used up?
I hope to enjoy that feeling again before too long.
Someone put that book there after the murder, to make it look as if he'd been reading when he was killed.
These chairs have the great advantage of being much cheaper than conventional ones.
You think if those people still have him they'll keep him alive?

as pronouns You can also use 'this', 'these', 'that', and 'those' as pronouns.

Is this really necessary?
Matters like these are always discussed in person.
What's wrong with that?
There won't be many businessmen queuing up for one of those.

agreement When used as pronouns, and as the subject of a sentence, 'this' and 'that' are followed by a singular verb, 'these' and 'those' by a plural verb.

This is what we did.
That was many years ago.
These have always been favourite animals of mine.
Those are business secrets.

as object or complement When pronouns, demonstratives can be used as the subject of a verb, as above, or as the object.

Have you got that?
Let me take these back to the lab.

Uses as determiners and pronouns

However, they are not used as a complement of verbs like 'be'. You cannot say, for example, 'my friend is that', or 'my book is this'. But you can use demonstratives in this way when something is being anticipated.

The other thing that bothers me is <u>this</u>. Where's the stamp?

referring to people

Generally you cannot use demonstratives as pronouns to refer to human beings. If you say 'I don't like that' you are talking about a thing, not a person. However, when you are introducing or identifying people (or asking about their identity) it is normal to use these words as pronouns.

'<u>This</u> is Mr Coyne,' said Philip.
'Who is <u>that</u>?' I whispered. '<u>That</u> is Geoff.'

on the telephone

There is one difference between American and British usage here. When asking about someone's identity on the telephone, it is normal to say 'Who is this?' in American English. In British English you can say 'Who is that?' though this might sound slightly abrupt, and 'Who is there?' or 'Who is speaking?' might be preferred.

'that of' 'those of'

Sometimes 'that' and 'those' do not have the idea of 'distance'; that is, they do not have any demonstrative idea. This is often the case when they are followed by 'of'.

The only sound was <u>that of</u> a car.
His eyes seemed to bulge like <u>those of</u> a toad.
The mental abilities of apes are markedly superior to <u>those of</u> monkeys.

This is a formal usage. It is something like saying 'the one of' or 'the ones of'.

'those who' 'those which'

Similarly, 'those' has no idea of distance when it is followed by a relative clause beginning with words such as 'which' or 'who'.

The market favoured <u>those who</u> had property and discriminated against <u>those who</u> did not.

Chapter 3

> *You are asked to indicate <u>those which</u> most describe your personality.*

Sometimes the relative clause comes after an apparent quantifier construction with 'of'.

> *Apologies to <u>those of you who</u> wrote in to complain.*
> *<u>Those of the inhabitants who</u> can do so escape to the more congenial lowland climate.*

Again it is formal. 'Those' can also be followed by other types of qualification.

> *He was not among <u>those crying</u>.*
> *<u>Those determined to kill</u> can always find suitable opportunities.*

In both the above examples, 'those' is understood as referring to people; this is often the case with these uses of 'those'.

'that which' 'That' can be followed by 'which', but it is very formal.

> *They say the only real knowledge is <u>that which</u> can be measured.*
> *<u>That which</u> an individual seeks, that he will find.*

as non-demonstrative determiners Sometimes when 'that' or 'those' are determiners and are followed by a relative clause there is also no demonstrative idea.

> *I speak of the richness and ambiguity of experience, including <u>that experience which is inherent in art</u>.*
> *He said that among <u>those people they questioned</u> was his bodyguard.*
> *He is richly endowed with <u>those qualities that make a good parliamentarian</u>.*

In these examples, 'that' and 'those' are simply a more formal way of saying 'the'.

before 'one' and 'ones' An alternative to using 'this', 'that', 'these', and 'those' as pronouns is to put 'one' or 'ones' after them. If you say 'this one' or 'that one' you are telling your listener to look for a singular referent (often a noun phrase with the indefinite article).

The difference in meaning between 'this' and 'that'

The first few hours of a fete are usually the busiest, and this one was no exception.
A kid had shown me how to open a lock as simple as this one with a bent wire.
We'll get back to you on that one.

'That one' here probably means a question that has been asked.

If you say 'these ones' or 'those ones' you are talking about something plural.

Some birds eat seeds but look at these ones carefully.
How did those ones die?

before numbers 'These' and 'those' are often followed by numbers, which can be either determiners or pronouns.

These three men are between thirty and fifty.
She'll make short work of those two.

'This' and 'that' can also be followed by 'one' and then a noun.

Twenty-five thousand of them came down the river in that one year.

'One' is emphatic here.

after 'all', 'both', 'half' Demonstratives can occur after 'all', 'both', and 'half'.

She's jolly lucky getting all that money
He's been out in Ceylon all these years.
There is probably some truth in both these theories.
More than half this land is unused.

Alternatives are possible with 'of': 'all of that money', 'all of these years', 'both of these theories', 'half of this land'.

3.2 The difference in meaning between **this** and **that**, and **these** and **those**

different types of closeness The difference in meaning between **this** (plural **these**) and **that** (plural **those**) is usually described in terms of closeness and distance to the speaker or writer. If something is close to you, you should use 'this' or

Chapter 3

'these', and if it is not you should use 'that' or 'those'. This is a simple way of explaining the difference but it does not give the whole picture. There are many situations where the use of 'this' or 'that' has nothing to do with physical closeness. For instance, look at the way 'these' is used in the following example:

Another occupant of the hedgerow is the hedgehog. These have always been favourite animals of mine.

Here the speaker is talking about 'hedgehogs'. They are 'close' because they were mentioned in the previous sentence.

There are several ways in which the idea of closeness can occur. Here are some of them.

- Closeness in space

If something is physically near to you, you can use **this** or **these**; if not, **that** or **those**. This is obviously more important when you are speaking.

No one had worked in this place for ages.
A lot of these houses round here have glass in the front doors.
I think we're going to have some nice plums on that tree.
I don't like the look of those clouds.

related to 'here' and 'there'

'This' and 'these' can be compared to 'here', while 'that' and 'those' can be related to 'there'. Particularly in informal spoken English, it is quite common to find 'this' or 'these' in the same sentence as 'here'; likewise, you often find 'that' or 'those' in the same sentence as 'there'.

How about this gentleman here?
I am so sorry your stay here has coincided with all this trouble.
See that redhead over there?
The key to the mystery lay there, hidden behind that bush.

The difference in meaning between 'this' and 'that'

'yon' In some dialects of English, particularly Scottish, there is the word **yon**, which can be used like 'that' to talk about something distant from the speaker. It is used with both singular and plural nouns.

You mean you'll take yon old tub out in this weather?
...one of yon fancy foreign lagers.

'yonder' **Yonder** is occasionally found in very formal, archaic English, referring to something distant from both speaker and hearer.

Pray advance thy horse beyond yonder ditch.

If 'that' were used in this situation, it might suggest that the ditch was near to the person being addressed.

'them' **Them**, which is usually a personal object pronoun, is also used instead of 'those' in non-standard English.

Did you really see them things like you said?

- Closeness in time

'This' and 'that' are very useful for showing how events relate to the point in time that the writer or speaker is particularly concerned with.

'that' for past You use **that** for events in the past; it has the idea of something which is finished.

Sometimes I've wondered what she really believed about that accident.
At that point he became worried.

'this' for present and future **This** is used for events that are still taking place, or about to take place at the time of speaking.

This party is really boring.
And this party will be all snobs.
This is how you begin.

In this last example 'this' refers to a future event – something that the speaker is about to demonstrate.

Chapter 3

related to 'now' and 'then'

The difference between 'this' and 'that' is parallel to the difference between 'now' and 'then' (when it is used as an adverb of time). And there is a tendency to use past tenses with 'that', and present tense forms with 'this'.

This is now a very serious and interesting affair.
Well, I paid for that decision back then.

past tense with 'this'

However, this does not mean that you cannot use the past tense with 'this'.

His recovery this time was slower.
By this time she was married to her third husband.

Using 'this' shows that even though the time is in the past, it is the writer's current point of narration. Compare this with the following example.

I saw the Baileys frequently at that time.

Here the writer is talking about a time which is distant from his or her current viewpoint.

present tense with 'that'

Similarly, it is possible to use 'that' with the present tense.

Now imagine that you are one of your parents and that you are present at that party.

Here the speaker wants to suggest a distance from the party because it is not actually taking place.

'this' with time periods

When used in front of words denoting specific periods of time, such as *morning, night, day, week,* or *year,* 'this' generally refers to present or future events.

This week, and for the next eight weeks, there is a $10,000 first prize.

But it can also refer to past events if the period includes the present time.

This week Michael Jackson arrived at Heathrow airport to star in a new film.
The bank's branches in London have seen a large increase in the number of robberies this year.

The difference in meaning between 'this' and 'that'

You can use 'this' with *morning* and *afternoon* when they are past, but when it is still the same day.

The letter from the school came this morning.

'that' with time periods

You can use 'that' to talk about time periods which are related to a point in the past.

He had not suggested coming to the hotel for dinner that evening.
That night the gunfire in the east sounded louder.

'these days'

'These days' is a very common way of saying 'nowadays' or 'recently'.

These days the Olympics must mean the best.
He's been going out a lot more these days.

- Closeness inside a text

This is the most common use of demonstratives. Here **this**, **that**, **these**, and **those** are used to point to, or refer to, something elsewhere in the same text.

Her crew had found 306 bodies. Of these, 116 had been buried at sea.

Here 'these' is referring back to the noun group '306 bodies' in the previous sentence.

referring back and forward

Demonstratives usually refer to something already mentioned, as above. But they can sometimes refer forwards in anticipation.

This is what he says of his early silence:...

Here 'this' is referring to what comes next (represented by the three dots); the colon (:) makes the reference clear.

Often tense shows whether 'this' is referring backwards or forwards.

This chapter describes the contents of the annual report.
This chapter has been about relaxation training.

Chapter 3

referring to more than a noun

Often 'this' and 'that' refer to more than just a noun group. They can refer to an idea contained in the previous sentence or paragraph.

They'd been shocked by what she had to tell them, and you couldn't blame them for <u>that</u>.

Here 'that' refers to their being shocked.

In formal and academic writing, it is very common to use 'this' as a determiner or pronoun to talk about an idea mentioned in a previous sentence. By using 'this' the writer can turn a complicated idea into a simple noun group which can then be talked about in the next sentence. A number of nouns are very common in this situation, for example *claim, belief, idea, problem,* and *theory.*

Analysis of the rock from this huge crater shows that it is most likely the result of a gigantic impact. <u>This belief</u> is strengthened by close similarities between the rock and glass beads found in Haiti.

The smaller the company the harder it is for them to devote time and money to increasing efficiency. Successful nations recognised <u>this problem</u> long ago.

Here the belief and the problem are described in the whole of the previous sentence.

'in this way'

'In this way' is another way of referring back to some idea or method mentioned before.

This is the first time drug tests have been carried out and he has the dubious honour of being the first athlete to be banned <u>in this way</u>.

Once your test has been assessed, you will receive a cassette at the appropriate level of the language. <u>In this way</u>, you can start preparing for the course before you leave home.

Other ways of using 'this' and 'that'

- Closeness in feeling

'that' and 'those' for negative ideas

'That' and 'those' are often used with words that express a negative emotion.

That stupid bus broke down not long after we left.
I'm not going in the sea round those nasty rocks.

Using 'that' and 'those' makes the feeling stronger than 'the stupid bus' or 'your nasty rocks'. Sometimes 'that' is enough to show the negative idea.

But what was Edwin doing bringing that man along?

But of course you can still say 'I like that idea', where you are being positive about something that is distant.

'this' in stories

In informal English, in storytelling or jokes, you often find **this** where you would expect 'a' when something is being introduced. It is used when something is familiar to the speaker and soon will be familiar to the listener.

Anyway, there's this woman in my life. Known her for a long time.
Then there was this loud clatter as it fell off.

3.3 Other ways of using **this** and **that**

as intensifiers

You can use **this** and **that** as adverbs to modify adjectives. Such adverbs are sometimes called intensifiers.

Will it always be this hot?
It was a superb game. It is a credit to the players that they could produce that good a match.

The meaning is similar to 'so' or 'as' but it is more precise; there is usually something you are making a comparison with. 'This hot' has the idea 'as hot as it is now'; 'that good' suggests 'as good as people say it is'. Sometimes if you stress 'that' you are being more general; if you say 'It isn't that difficult', you are just comparing with a high level of difficulty.

She was troubled by the feeling that she hadn't stood

Chapter 3

up well to the doctor, who wasn't all <u>that good</u> a surgeon.

in expressions 'This' and, more frequently, 'that' are found as pronouns in a number of expressions.

You can put **at that** after a phrase which modifies or emphasizes something said before.

'I do look forward to working on that puzzle some more.'—'It might be fun, <u>at that</u>.'

You can use **that is** (followed by a comma) when you want to make a previous statement clearer. It is like saying 'in other words' or 'i.e.'

We're taking care of his cat while he's in jail. <u>That is</u>, Freddy's in jail, not the cat.

You can use **that's it** to show agreement with something that someone has said.

'You mean an enemy agent?'—'<u>That's it</u>.'

You can also use it to say that someone has had enough of something.

<u>That's it</u>! Either he goes or I do.

Or it can mean that something is finished.

I think <u>that's it</u> for tonight, gentlemen.

You can also use **that's that** to show that a topic is finished.

I'll attend the rehearsals and <u>that's that</u>.

This means a decision has been made and no more discussion is allowed.

You can use **this and that** to avoid giving details about something.

He gave her a whisky and soda and chatted about <u>this and that</u>.
'What was stolen?'—'Oh, <u>this and that</u>.'

Personal pronouns as demonstratives

For the meaning of **that's all**, see **7.3**.

with 'kind' and 'sort'

You can put 'kind of' or 'sort of' and a noun after 'this' or 'that'. (Or 'kinds of' or 'sorts of' after 'these' or 'those'.)

My own view is that <u>this kind of</u> store, <u>these kinds of</u> supermarkets, have been around long enough for us to get used to them.
<u>That kind of</u> belief is not at all unusual.
He doesn't want <u>that sort of</u> publicity.
Good businesses have been doing <u>these sorts of</u> things for years.

The meaning is similar to 'such' or 'such a'. In the above examples, you could say 'such a store', 'such supermarkets', 'such a belief', 'such publicity', or 'such things' without changing the meaning. See Chapter 11 for more information on 'such'.

WARNING

It is important to distinguish the use of 'that' as a determiner and pronoun from its uses as a relative pronoun and conjunction. These uses are both very common.

It was a word <u>that</u> appealed to the new writers of a new age.
Yet Morton seemed to know <u>that</u> I'd been there.

Here there is no idea of 'demonstrating' anything.

The same is true with 'so that' and 'so...that', which are conjunctions indicating a result.

The boot has been enlarged <u>so that</u> it is almost 5ft 8in long.
The car that struck her was going <u>so</u> fast <u>that</u> the impact sent her flying.

3.4 Personal pronouns as demonstratives

So far we have looked at cases where things are being pointed to that are close to speakers or listeners, or far from both. But what if it is the speakers or listeners who are being pointed to? In this case you can use

Chapter 3

personal pronouns in front of nouns as demonstratives.

'we' or 'us' for speakers

If speakers want to refer to themselves, you can put **we** or **us** before the noun.

We're a selfish lot, we writers.
I heard my parents talking of sending us children away.

'We' is used when the noun is subject, and 'us' when the noun is object or comes after a preposition.

We lawyers are paid to take the tough choices.
I hope you don't expect us girls to do the cooking.
The majority of us lads are professional drivers.

You cannot use 'me' or 'I' in this way, or indeed any other personal pronouns.

'you' for listeners

To refer to your listeners, you can use **you** followed by a noun.

I think you fellows are far too modest.
What's the matter with you people?

This is only possible in the plural. You cannot say 'What's the matter with you fellow?'

In **3.2** a similar, but non-standard, use with **them**, to refer to people or things that are not close to listener or speaker, was noted.

4 'Wh'-word determiners

what, which, whose

This chapter discusses some members of a group of very common words that are used in a number of similar ways. This group also includes important words such as 'when', 'where', 'why', and 'how'. We call the members of this group *'wh'-words* because they all start with those letters (except 'how'). Typically we think of them as question words, but in fact they are more common in other uses.

Three of them are of interest here because they can be used as determiners: **what**, **which**, and **whose**. Their meanings and uses are dealt with below. Chapter 11 describes another use of 'what': when it is used in exclamations.

In addition, this chapter looks at the similar uses of these words, and the way their meaning is changed, when they are combined with the suffix '-ever'.

These words are described below in the following sections:

    4.1 General uses of 'wh'-word determiners
    4.2 In questions: **what, which, whose**
    4.3 In relative clauses: **which, whose**
    4.4 In noun clauses: **what, which, whose**
    4.5 Uses of **whatever, whichever, whoever's**

4.1 General uses of 'wh'-word determiners

with count and uncount nouns

'Wh'-word determiners can be used with all sorts of noun: singular and plural count nouns and uncount nouns.

What answer do you give to a question like that?
What colours did you see?
People don't actually know what information they want.

Chapter 4

Which paper did you read this in?
I don't need to talk about which situations these practical skills were taught in.
And whose side are you on?
It is still unclear why the bombs were detonated, or on exactly whose orders.
He is a writer whose humor is not without substance.

'which' as quantifier

Which (but not **what**) can be a quantifier.

Which of these statements comes closest to your view?
We are trying to find out which of the existing rules will apply.
I didn't care which of us won.

In this respect, 'which' is an exception to the general rule against using definite determiners with definite noun groups (see **1.6**).

'what' and 'which' as pronouns

'What' and 'which' are used very often as pronouns; in fact, they are far more common as pronouns than as determiners.

What concerned him more was his present position.
All of us know what the reason is.
What is the status of a poet in society?
What steps are involved? Which are crucial?
He did not even know which was Mrs Hanson's hotel room.
This is a feeling which we can never know.
This may not be the only criterion by which decisions are reached.

'which one'

In direct and indirect questions, instead of 'which' as a pronoun you can say 'which one' (singular) or 'which ones' (plural). This sounds more emphatic.

One of them isn't. Would you feel confident in predicting which one?
In the photo was Marko Vukcic, holding a rifle loosely at his side. 'Which one's your uncle?' I asked.
Try a few different methods and see which ones help most.

General uses of 'wh'-word determiners

'Which one' can also make it clear when you are talking about only one item in a group.

I draw on your fingers and toes, and you have to work out which one I'm touching.

'whose' as pronoun

Whose is relatively rare as a pronoun.

I knew whose it was.
Whose is the boat?

meaning of 'what' and 'which'

As was said in **1.3**, the difference between 'what' and 'which' is that 'which' picks out something (or some things) from a group which the listener or reader is familiar with; this is not the case with 'what'.

Which idea do you think is best?
What colours did you see?

In the first example 'which idea' means one from a known (and limited) group of ideas; 'what' is vaguer and does not suggest an established group. However, the difference is not always precise.

They determine what type of plants the virus can infect and which insects can carry the virus.

Here perhaps the difference is that the writer wants to suggest that the range of plants is broader than the range of insects.

referring to people or things

You can use both 'what' and 'which' as determiners to refer to people or things.

They have a responsibility to discover which wives have walked out on their husbands.
Which party will you vote for in the election?
In what manner was she living?
What person in his right mind would go for that?

As a pronoun 'what' cannot have a human interpretation.

What could it be?

Chapter 4

'Whose' can occasionally refer to things, not people.

More framed photographs decorate <u>a side table whose</u> cover matches the floral curtains.

meaning of 'whose'

In meaning, 'whose' is like the possessive determiners ('my', 'your', etc) described in Chapter 2. It helps to relate a noun to a person; in questions (see **4.2**), the person is unknown, while in relative clauses (see **4.3**), it is the person just mentioned.

<u>Whose money</u> were they wasting?
He picks up <u>a stranger whose</u> car has broken down.

However, the relationship is not only one of possession as in the examples above; it can involve different kinds of association, such as family relations and personal characteristics.

Mary is an orphan <u>whose parents</u> tragically died.
One of the Britons, <u>whose identity</u> has not been revealed, was taken to hospital.

It can also show an underlying verbal relationship, especially where the person involved would be the subject of a verb.

Now was not the time to start thinking of mother, <u>whose death</u> had so distressed me.
He stars as a young stranger in town, <u>whose arrival</u> is followed by some mysterious deaths.
Wolves are highly social animals <u>whose success</u> depends upon cooperation.

In these examples, there is the idea that 'mother died', 'a young stranger arrived', and 'wolves succeed'.

'what kind of' 'what sort of'

'What' is often used in front of 'kind of' and 'sort of', or 'kinds of' and 'sorts of'. (See also **3.3**.)

Tell me <u>what kind of</u> jacket you want.
<u>What sort of</u> music did they play?
<u>What kinds of</u> things did you spend your money on each week?
<u>What sorts of</u> excuses do they give for his behaviour?

WARNING

In pronunciation 'whose' sounds the same as "who's"

In relative clauses: 'which', 'whose'

(short for 'who is' or 'who has'). It is important not to confuse them when writing.

4.2 In questions: what, which, whose

What, **which**, and **whose** occur as determiners in noun groups which are the focus of questions. In direct questions, they usually, but not always, occur first in the sentence.

<u>What number</u> is that?
<u>What effect</u> would success have on my self-esteem?
The question remains, to <u>what extent</u> are they true?
<u>Which idea</u> do you think is best?
<u>Which friends</u> would you want to see?
<u>Which chair company</u> did he work for?
<u>Whose idea</u> was it you should have it?
On <u>whose authority</u> can we act?

indirect questions 'What', 'which', and 'whose' also occur in what are called *indirect questions*. Strictly speaking, these are not questions; they do not have a question mark at the end because they are only part of a larger sentence.

I wonder <u>what book I'll read tonight before I go to sleep</u>.
They ask <u>which car is worth what</u>.

These are discussed in more detail in **4.4** below.

4.3 In relative clauses: which, whose

Which and **whose** are both used frequently in relative clauses. A clause is a group of words which has all the elements necessary for a sentence, namely a subject, a verb, and other parts, but which is part of a larger sentence. Relative clauses are clauses which give extra information about a preceding noun group. They come after the noun group, and 'which' or 'whose' is at the start or near the start of the clause.

'which' as relative pronoun As a relative pronoun, 'which' is very common.

It was the moment <u>which</u> launched his campaign of conquest.

Here 'which' refers to 'moment'.

Chapter 4

'which' as determiner

'Which' can sometimes occur as a relative determiner when there is a preposition in front.

The programme will continue until 1994 <u>by which time</u> $3 million will have been spent.

'which' referring to a clause

'Which' can be used in another type of relative clause, something that is sometimes called a ***sentential relative***. Here it does not refer back to the preceding noun group but to the whole idea contained in the previous clause. 'Which' is typically a pronoun in this situation.

I told her she didn't have to do that, <u>which</u> sounds like an ungrateful thing to say.
Every soldier was wearing earplugs, <u>which</u> made conversation difficult.

In this example 'which' refers to the fact that the soldiers were wearing earplugs.

'Which' is possible as a determiner in this situation if it has a preposition before it, but it sounds formal.

It was derived from Posidonius, <u>for which reason</u> much of its information may well have been out-of-date.

However, 'in which case' is a common expression.

Sometimes feta is very salty, <u>in which case</u> no salt needs to be added.

In some old texts you may find sentential 'which' being used as a determiner without a preposition.

He then resolved to leave, <u>which decision</u> pleased me greatly.

But this kind of use is extremely rare in modern English.

'whose' as determiner

'Whose' is often used as a determiner to introduce relative clauses.

They have collected a petition from 1500 other parents <u>whose children</u> are forced to do games against their will.

In noun clauses: 'what', 'which', 'whose'

His first love was a Chinese girl <u>whose family</u> ran a shop opposite his home.

In these cases, 'whose' is referring back to '1500 other parents' and 'a Chinese girl'. 'Whose' does not occur as a relative pronoun.

'Whose' often comes after a preposition.

If you happen to be the farmer <u>on whose</u> land the birds arrive then it's a very serious problem.

You can also use it in a quantifier construction, for example after 'many of', 'most of', or 'some of'.

It would mean giving more power to Congress, <u>many of whose</u> members are widely believed to be corrupt.
British tax law is hard on companies <u>most of whose</u> earnings come from abroad.

Other words which can be used to introduce relative clauses (but only as pronouns) are 'that', 'who', and 'whom'.

WARNING 'What' is not used to introduce relative clauses. You cannot say 'This is something what I like very much'. However, section **4.4** below describes a use of 'what' which is similar to relative clauses.

4.4 In noun clauses: **what, which, whose**

Section **4.3** described relative clauses, which are part of a noun group. There is another type of clause which takes the place of noun groups in the sentence; these are sometimes called ***noun clauses*** (or ***nominal clauses***). Noun clauses function as one element of a sentence, for example a subject or an object. One way of introducing them is with a 'wh'-word such as **what**, **which**, or **whose**.

object noun clauses Most commonly these words come at the start of a noun clause which is the object of a sentence.

As children we knew <u>what colours we liked</u>.
I will tell you <u>what number I'm ringing from</u>.
I didn't know <u>which channel I was tuned to</u>.

Chapter 4

> *Check which side is tightest.*
> *I do not know whose idea this was.*
> *His girlfriend persuaded the two men to race to see whose car was fastest.*

Occasionally the clause comes after a preposition.

> *You can see into which category you currently fall.*

subject noun clauses

The clause can also be the subject of a sentence.

> *What we need at this difficult time is a bit of tolerance and commonsense.*

However, this is not normal with 'which'. This is because it is more usual to use a construction with 'it' as the subject and the clause at the end, especially if the clause is long.

> *It will soon be clear which firms start sliding towards bankruptcy.*

You could also say 'Which firms start sliding towards bankruptcy will soon be clear', but this would sound a little clumsy.

implied questions

This use is typical with certain verbs, for example *ask, decide, discover, find out, guess, know, prove, say, see, tell*, and *wonder*. Very often there is a question that is implied, like the indirect questions in **4.2**.

> *No prize for guessing which side is likely to prevail.*

Here there is the idea that someone has asked, or might ask, 'Which side is likely to prevail?', but this is not necessarily the case.

> *They took what they could get.*

as pronouns

'What' and 'which' can also be pronouns in indirect and implied questions.

> *But that was not really what occupied his mind.*
> *You don't know which is which, do you?*

Here the 'wh'-word can be understood as 'the thing that (occupied his mind)'.

Uses of 'whatever', 'whichever', 'whoever's'

4.5 Uses of **whatever, whichever, whoever's**

Most 'wh'-words can be combined with '-ever' to make compounds such as 'whatever', 'whenever', and 'wherever'. One use of these words is to suggest that the precise answer to the question implied by the basic 'wh'-word is unimportant or does not matter. So if you say 'Whatever you do, you lose', it means 'It doesn't matter what you do, you lose' or 'Regardless of what you do, you lose'. 'Any' can have a similar meaning (see **7.9**); if you say 'I'll answer whatever questions they ask', you could also say 'I'll answer any questions they ask'.

in noun clauses **Whatever** and **whichever** can be determiners in this situation. They introduce noun clauses like those in **4.4** above.

You just have to make a serious start yourself with whatever resources you have available.
He remains unprepared for whatever problems lie ahead.
I'll be able to afford whatever fee you ask.
Both sides have agreed to recognise whichever group wins a majority vote.

The clause often has the function of an adverb in the sentence.

It never looked any better whichever way I looked at it.
Whichever direction he came from he still arrived at the same point.

'Whatever' and 'whichever' can also be pronouns, and 'whichever' can be a quantifier.

He tried to do whatever they wanted.
Whichever he chooses, he is damned.
Whichever of us survives, will do so for us both.

Whoever's, the '-ever'-word corresponding to 'whose', is rarely used.

These are mostly vegetarian meals cooked by whoever's turn it is that day.

Chapter 4

Whoever's this is is going to have fun.

special uses of 'whatever'

'Whatever' has a number of special uses.

It can occur in a 'clause' which has no verb.

He'll come whatever the weather.
Whatever your reasons, I'm grateful.

Here you could also say 'whatever the weather is' or 'whatever your reasons are'.

You can use 'or whatever' at the end of a sentence to show vagueness in speech, especially after a list of possibilities.

He's won a car or a holiday or whatever.

You can use 'whatever' to make the force of a question greater, to show surprise or annoyance.

Whatever is the world coming to?

You can use 'whatever' after a noun following a negative or another non-assertive word (see **1.8**). You use it for emphasis; it is similar to saying 'at all'.

It made no sense whatever.

5 Numbers and similar determiners

one, two, three, etc

first, second, third, etc

twice, three times, etc

half, a third, two-fifths, etc

The most obvious way to 'determine' a noun is to state the quantity of it involved. Chapters 6 and onwards deal with words such as 'some', 'all', 'many', and 'few', which you can use when talking about quantities when you are not sure about, or do not want to state, the exact number involved. This chapter deals with the opposite case, when you do know the number or amount involved.

This chapter deals with open classes of words like cardinal and ordinal numbers, fractions, and multipliers, which can be used to state a precise number or amount of something. Two very important words, 'one' and 'half', are given extra treatment here because of the many different ways in which they are used and the difficulties they can present to learners.

These words are dealt with in the following sections:

    5.1 Cardinal numbers: **one, two, three,** etc
    5.2 Special uses of **one**
    5.3 Ordinal numbers: **first, second, third,** etc
    5.4 Multipliers: **twice, three times,** etc
    5.5 Fractions: **a third, two-fifths,** etc
    5.6 Uses of **half**

5.1 Cardinal numbers: **one, two, three,** etc

The numbers **one, two, three,** and so on, are sometimes called *cardinal numbers* to distinguish them from ordinal numbers (see **5.3** below). You can use them as determiners, quantifiers, or pronouns.

She hadn't had a bite to eat in <u>three days</u>.
There were <u>four of them</u>, two police cars and two others.
The <u>seven freckles</u> had increased to <u>ten</u>.

'a' or 'one' before 'hundred', etc

You must put **a** or **one** (or another number) in front of **hundred**, **thousand**, and **million**. 'One' usually has more emphasis than 'a'.

The book sold over <u>a million</u> copies.
He weighed at least <u>one hundred</u> pounds less.

In the middle of numbers only 'one' is possible: 'three thousand, *one* hundred and twenty' (3,120).

plurals of 'hundred', etc

After another number you do not use the plurals of 'hundred', 'thousand', and 'million'.

I hear they're expecting <u>five thousand</u> demonstrators.
He was prepared to pay <u>two million</u>.

'Tens', 'hundreds', 'thousands', and 'millions' can be used for vague quantities.

<u>Millions</u> of jobs are likely to be lost.

use of the hyphen

You should use a hyphen when writing compound numbers: 'twenty-one', 'seventy-five'.

'and' in long numbers

In British English, 'and' is used before the last two figures of a long number: '475' is spoken (and written in full) as 'four hundred and seventy-five'. In American English, 'and' can be left out.

after other determiners

When used with other determiners, numbers almost always come afterwards. You can use numbers after definite determiners when it is known what you are talking about.

They form an indivisible whole, like <u>the two sides</u> of a coin.
He said <u>the two of you</u> were very close.
He took special delight in <u>his three</u> daughters.

Cardinal numbers: 'one', 'two', 'three', etc

Numbers can also come after some indefinite determiners such as 'all', 'any', 'every', and 'some'.

All three policemen moved as one.
Any four out of the five would make a potential medal-winning team.
Take a little fruit every three or four hours.
He started drinking heavily, some three years after we'd married.

Here 'every' refers to a repeated event (see **7.5**). 'Some', when it is used in this way, has the meaning of 'approximately' (see **6.2**).

use with 'other' Numbers can be used before and after 'other', but there can be a difference in meaning. When you put numbers first without an article, 'other' distinguishes the noun that follows from similar things that have already been mentioned.

Two other Australian diplomats were also killed in the incident.
He would plead guilty to at least one other offence.
Mary rents a house with three other girls.

In this last example, 'other' distinguishes the three girls from Mary.

You cannot put 'other' in front of a number unless there is another determiner first, such as 'the', 'this', or 'my'. When you say 'the other three' it has the idea of 'the remaining three'.

The faces of the other three girls were fixed on Alex.

It is also possible to say 'the three other' with the same meaning, though this is less common.

Police took the three other canoeists to hospital.

If there is no noun following you must put 'other' before the number.

Thirty-two went into uniform. The other three went into the coal mines.

You could not say 'the three other', but it is possible to say 'the three others'.

Chapter 5

If you say, for example, 'another three' it can mean an additional three.

They drove for <u>another three</u> hours.
China picked up <u>another ten</u> gold medals.

For the order of cardinal numbers with ordinal numbers, see **5.3** below.

special pronoun uses

As a pronoun, a number can often mean the hour of the day.

The helicopter lifted off just after <u>four</u>.

This means four o'clock. Numbers on their own can also indicate ages.

So you must have gone to school at about <u>six</u>.
What else could a girl of <u>twelve</u> want?

This means the age of six or twelve.

as nouns

Numbers can be used as nouns, in the singular or plural, for example when referring to playing cards or banknotes.

And then I gave you <u>a fifty</u>.
He pulled a wad of mixed notes from his pants pocket, <u>fives</u> and <u>tens</u>.
He turned his cards over. A king and two <u>fives</u>.

Plural numbers can also be used to refer to groups of people.

The guests left in <u>ones and twos</u>.

'twenties', 'thirties', etc

You can put 'the' in front of **twenties**, **thirties**, etc (also written **20's**, **30's**) to talk about a period of ten years in a century.

In <u>the twenties and thirties</u>, my grandfather had a sawmill on his farm.
He was a superstar of <u>the Fifties</u>.

And you can use a possessive determiner in the same way for someone's age.

She left Wales in <u>her twenties</u> and never went back.

Cardinal numbers: 'one', 'two', 'three', etc

This means that she was between 20 and 29 years old when she left Wales.

See **5.2** below for uses of 'ones'.

in compounds Numbers are common in compound adjectives.

This is the first of a <u>three-volume</u> series.
I am working a <u>ten-hour</u> day.
It was a <u>one-storey</u> house.
A <u>one per cent rise</u> would be a disaster.

modified by adverbs Numbers are often modified by adverbs such as 'over', 'more than', 'less than', 'only', 'nearly', 'almost', 'about', and 'around'.

His majority was <u>over eighteen thousand</u>.
I was in a car accident <u>more than twenty</u> years ago.
I can have an ambulance here in <u>less than five</u> minutes.
<u>Only two</u> men were saved.
He knew they were <u>nearly fifty</u> miles beyond the valley.
It was <u>almost ten</u> minutes since either of them had spoken.
<u>About a hundred</u> other people had had the same idea.
In the south of England temperatures have reached <u>around thirty</u> degrees.

'one or two' You can be less precise about a number by using phrases such as 'one or two' or 'two or three'.

They are clearly talking to <u>one or two</u> people.
He suggested his departure should be postponed by another <u>two or three</u> days.
There were only <u>twenty or thirty</u> such factories in the British Isles.

'a couple'
'a dozen'
'a score'

Some other words can be used as nouns to indicate numerical amounts, such as **a couple** (two), **a dozen** (twelve), and **a score** (twenty). All of them can be used to indicate vague or approximate amounts; 'a couple' often suggests more than two. Of these words, 'a dozen' can be used as a determiner, as can 'a couple' in spoken American English.

I watched the replay <u>a dozen times</u> this morning.
I haven't shaved for <u>a couple days</u>.

Chapter 5

'A couple' and 'a score' can be used before 'of'.

He didn't say much, a couple of sentences.
The Tuscan coastline has a score of popular resorts.

The plural forms 'dozens' and 'scores' are also common in front of 'of' to talk about a large number.

Dozens of journalists have descended upon Mostar.
Amnesty International has now interviewed scores of witnesses.

5.2 Special uses of **one**

One is used in a number of different ways when it does not only have the idea of a number.

as indefinite pronoun
You can use it as an indefinite pronoun to avoid repeating a noun group with an indefinite article.

She aches for a child, he doesn't want one.

Here 'one' stands for 'a child'. But where the noun would no longer be indefinite, you use 'it'.

When a car hits clothing it leaves a mark.

with adjectives
If 'one' is modified with an adjective, you need to put 'a' or 'an' in front.

My father was a lawyer. A good one.

You use 'ones' for a plural noun after an adjective or with a following phrase.

There were small problems that had mounted up into big ones.
Breakfast cereals are a good source of fibre. Go for ones with ingredients that are wholegrains.

But you do not use 'ones' on its own for plurals. You cannot say 'We need ideas and he has ones'. Instead you can say 'He has some'.

'the one'
You can use 'one' (or 'ones') with 'the' to pick out something already known or established.

What, a mill? Like the one at Bridgend?

Special uses of 'one'

Peacocks are the males of the species, <u>the ones</u> with the fabulous feathers.

This is very common before a relative clause.

That's <u>the one</u> I want.

emphatic use
You can use 'the' or another definite determiner before 'one' and a noun to emphasize 'one' as a number.

I remembered <u>the one time</u> I had failed to heed the warning.
<u>My one idea</u> was to get out of that place.

This has the idea of 'only'.

after other determiners
You use 'one' after many other determiners to form phrases that behave as pronouns: 'that one', 'these ones', 'any one', 'each one', 'every one', and so on. In most cases these are alternatives to pronoun uses (such as 'that' or 'these' on their own), although they may sound less formal. For more information on these uses see the relevant chapters.

'one...other'
When comparing two things, you can say 'one' followed, later in the sentence, by 'the other' or 'another'.

Jasmine has <u>one</u> leg slightly longer than <u>the other</u>.
The large suitcase was to <u>one</u> side, his typewriter on <u>the other</u>.
<u>One</u> person drums softly and <u>another</u> rattles.

with time periods
You can use 'one' with time periods in the past or future to suggest that the precise moment or period is not important.

I asked him <u>one morning</u> if he had slept well.
<u>One day</u> he might become Minister of the Interior.

as emphatic form of 'a'
In many cases 'one' is used as an emphatic form of the indefinite article. In informal speech, you can use 'one' before a noun group referring to something impressive, remarkable, or shocking.

Chapter 5

> *It's like <u>one great big riot</u> from start to finish.*
> *That's <u>one hell of a risk</u> to take.*

In formal language, 'one' before a name indicates someone possibly unknown who is being mentioned for the first time.

> *The villain on that occasion was <u>one Michael Thomas</u>.*

as personal pronoun 'One' can be used as a personal pronoun to make general statements.

> *<u>One</u> should never take 'no' for an answer.*

This is a formal use. 'You' can be used in the same way less formally.

in expressions 'One' is used in a number of expressions.

In spoken English you can use **one** to talk about jokes or stories.

> *Did you hear <u>the one</u> about the particle physicist?*
> *Heard <u>a good one</u> in the club the other day.*

You can use **for one** to express a personal opinion which you hope others might agree with.

> *I <u>for one</u> am sad that London Zoo is to close.*

If you say **for one thing**, you are giving one reason out of many for something.

> *He had failed to make his mark in television. He was too bad at political interviewing, <u>for one thing</u>.*

If you say somebody is **one for** something, or **a one for** something, it means they like it. It is usually used after a negative word.

> *She was never <u>a one for</u> dogma.*

You are a one, in informal English, is a way of scolding someone in an affectionate or humorous way.

> *Oh <u>you are a one</u>, aren't you.*

5.3 Ordinal numbers: **first**, **second**, **third**, etc

Ordinal numbers are numbers which show the position of something in an order.

His planning application was rejected for the fourth time.
When he slipped past, on the tenth of the 30 laps, the race was as good as over.
He could only finish fifth.

formation They are formed from cardinal numbers by adding -**th** to the end, for example, 'seven**th**', 'fourteen**th**', 'hundred**th**'.

There are several exceptions: **first** (from 'one'), **second** (from 'two'), **third** (from 'three'), **fifth** (from 'five'), **eighth** (from 'eight'), **ninth** (from 'nine'), **twelfth** (from 'twelve'), as well as the compounds of these numbers: **twenty-first** (from 'twenty-one'), **thirty-second** (from 'thirty-two'), and so on.

abbreviations You can write ordinal numbers as figures followed by their last two letters: **1st** (for 'first'), **2nd** for ('second'), **3rd** (for 'third'), **4th** (for 'fourth'), **5th** (for 'fifth'), **21st** (for 'twenty-first'), **100th** (for 'hundredth'), and so on.

as determiners and pronouns You can use ordinal numbers as determiners, and pronouns.

She was the first female sub-editor ever on a British newspaper.
The design is based on two assumptions. The first is that not all people have the same interests and abilities.

with 'the' and other definite determiners Ordinal numbers are usually used with 'the', as in the examples above, because, in most cases, it is already understood from the context or from general knowledge that there is a sequence of things to which the speaker is referring.

I had assembled a team of ten, but now had only nine. The tenth had fallen under a table.

Chapter 5

You can also use them with other definite determiners.

My first reaction was to hit him, but he was old. My second was to resign.
This fourth annual show is going to be our finest.

with 'a' However, there are many exceptions to this where you want to focus on a particular item that might not be expected from the context or general knowledge. In such cases you would use 'a' or 'an'.

His father had a first wife who died.
There was a third reason for haste.

'next' and 'last' Two other words, **next** and **last**, are like ordinal numbers in that they help to show the order of something. They also tend to be used with the definite article.

The next thing he heard was an insistent knocking on the door of his room.
Brenda took the last bite of her omelette.

However, in expressions like 'next week' and 'last night' there is usually no 'the'.

I'm going back next week.
Last month, IBM launched its most powerful mainframe computer to date.

with cardinal numbers When they are used with cardinal numbers, ordinals normally come first.

The student reads chemistry for the first two years.
The club is gripped mainly by the last three fingers of the left hand.

There are apparent exceptions to this where in fact the cardinal number is part of a compound adjective or noun.

Two first class stamps please.

The next example shows 'first' being used in both ways.

Multipliers: 'twice', 'three times', etc

They lost their first three first division fixtures.

in dates You also use ordinals in dates to express the day in a month. In British English, you can say, for example, 'March the first' or 'the first of March'; in American English 'March first' is more common. When writing it is more normal to use abbreviations: 'March 1st', or even 'March 1'.

Cardinal numbers are also used in fractions; for this, see **5.5** below.

5.4 Multipliers: **twice, three times**, etc

formation Multipliers are a group of words and phrases which you use to say that something is bigger in numerical terms than something you are comparing it to. Apart from **twice**, they are formed from numbers by adding 'times' (**three times, four times, a hundred times**, and so on).

And of course you get twice the profit.
The result is a brain three times the size of a human-sized ape.

In this situation **double** means the same as 'twice'.

Everything was almost double the normal price.

as predeterminers You use multipliers as predeterminers before 'the' and other definite determiners with nouns that indicate measures or amounts.

The bigger one is more than twice the size.
This will easily hold twice your weight.

You cannot use these words as quantifiers. You cannot say 'twice of the weight'.

'thrice' **Thrice** is an archaic way of saying 'three times'.

These enemies were serious men and women thrice his age.

as adverbs Multipliers are also used as adverbs.

Chapter 5

His mother married <u>twice</u>.

This means 'on two occasions'. With time periods you can use 'twice' or other multipliers before 'a' to talk about something that happens regularly.

He didn't have a regular housekeeper, just an old lady who came in <u>twice a week</u>.
This should be drunk <u>three times a day</u>.

These mean 'on two occasions in each week' and 'on three occasions in each day'.

before 'as' You can put 'as' after a multiplier to indicate the extent or factor by which something is being compared.

It weighs <u>twice as</u> much as a family car.
There are <u>five times as</u> many widows as widowers.
The fat cells in an obese person may be <u>100 times as</u> large as those in a thin person.

as adjectives Multipliers can become adjectives. They are hyphenated in this case.

The news will come as a relief to Prost, the <u>three-times</u> world champion.

'Twice' is found in compound adjectives.

Another hate was the <u>twice-weekly</u> inspections by the colonel.

5.5 Fractions: **a third**, **two-fifths**, etc

formation Fractions are 'numbers' that are smaller than one. They are used to express a proportion, that is, a part of something. They are composed of two parts: firstly, a cardinal number, or 'a', and then an ordinal number (or 'quarter').

Nearly <u>a third</u> of those asked gave no opinion.
Doctors fought to save him for <u>three quarters</u> of an hour.

Fractions usually have a hyphen but there is no strict rule about this.

Fractions: 'a third', 'two-fifths', etc

One-third of the awards have been given to women.
Today one third of the world's households are headed by women.

You do not use a hyphen after 'a' or 'an'.

You can say, for example, 'a third' or 'one third' but 'a' (or 'an') is far more common with all fractions of this kind.

I have written a quarter or a fifth of the book.

You can write fractions just using numbers: ½, ⅖. But the abbreviations that are common with cardinal numbers are not used with fractions; you cannot write 'one 3rd'.

plurals If the first number is more than one, then you must use a plural of the ordinal number.

They represented only two-fifths of the foreign population in 1982.
The fact remains that nine-tenths of women in this country do have children.

as quantifiers or predeterminers Fractions are very commonly used as quantifiers.

I paid $7,500 for a third of the business.

They are used as predeterminers only with nouns that indicate quantities.

The US emits eight times as much carbon dioxide as India, despite having less than a third the population.
He raced three-quarters the length of the pitch.

Often a comparison is involved.

Melbourne and Sydney had less than one-third the concentrations of sulphur dioxide found in New York and Tokyo.

before indefinite noun groups You can also put an indefinite noun group after 'of'.

Two-fifths of respondents want to work elsewhere.
About three quarters of visitors to the Disney parks in the US are over 18.

Chapter 5

pronouns

You can also use fractions like pronouns.

The content should be reduced by <u>one-third</u>, they recommended.
The discount rate is up by <u>three-quarters</u>.

'fourth' and 'quarter'

Fourth and **quarter** mean the same but 'quarter' is much more common in British English while 'fourth' is preferred in American English.

It said youngsters were responsible for <u>three-quarters</u> of car crime.
<u>Three fourths of all the lawyers in the world practice in the United States.</u>

'quarter' in times

You also use 'quarter' in stating a time 15 minutes before or after an hour. There are a number of possibilities. In British English you can say 'quarter to' and 'quarter past'. Some people put 'a' in front of 'quarter'. In American English you say 'a quarter of' and 'a quarter after'.

It was about <u>quarter to twelve</u> when she phoned. (11:45)
Nobody else turned up till <u>a quarter past ten</u>. (10:15)
Nancy glanced at her wristwatch. It showed <u>a quarter of two</u>. (1:45)
The time was recorded at <u>a quarter after five</u>. (5:15)

You can also say 'a quarter of an hour' to indicate a period of 15 minutes.

Within <u>a quarter of an hour</u> I was entering the woods.

'quarter' as a noun

'Quarter' has a number of special meanings as a noun, for example a fixed period of three months in a year.

Expectations of employment levels during the next <u>quarter</u> continue to worsen.

Or it can mean an American or Canadian coin worth 25 cents.

I dropped <u>a quarter</u> into the slot of the pay phone,

A 'quarter' can be a particular area in a town or city.

This <u>quarter</u> was rich in historical and literary associations.

Uses of 'half'

It can also refer in a general way to someone who is the source of something.

There was nothing to fear from that <u>quarter</u>.

5.6 Uses of **half**

as a quantifier

Half is a very interesting word because it can be used in so many ways. You can use it like other fractions, that is, as a quantifier with 'a' or 'one'. 'One' sounds more emphatic.

<u>One half of the park</u> consists of an excellent museum.
Nearly <u>a half of the army</u> remained in Britain.

You can also use 'half' as a quantifier without 'a' or 'one'.

<u>Half of the table</u> was concealed by a column.

difference between 'half' and 'a half'

'A half of the table' is also possible with a slightly different meaning; it has more the idea of a precise part, for example because the table can be divided in two.

The weather had been unexpectedly rough for nearly <u>a half of the</u> two-week winter cruise.

This refers to one continuous period of time. If you said 'for nearly half', this could mean that the weather was rough at different times.

before indefinite determiners

You can also say 'half of' in front of indefinite determiners.

Dina is not a solo performer but <u>half of a</u> double act.

You could also say 'a half of a' or 'one half of a'.

as a pronoun

When there is no noun following, 'a half' is more common than 'half' or 'one half'.

The proportion rose from a quarter to <u>a half</u>.

in numbers after 'and'

When 'half' comes at the end of numbers and other units (for example time periods) you must put 'and' and 'a' before it.

Chapter 5

The weight is about <u>four and a half</u> kilograms.
I must have slept three hours in the past <u>day and a half</u>.

You cannot say 'four and half'.

as predeterminer

You can also use 'half' as a predeterminer, that is, before another determiner.

<u>Half the building</u> was in flames.
That means you'll be there <u>half the night</u>.
More than <u>half this land</u> is unused.

There is no difference in meaning between this and saying 'half of this land' (to take the last example above). You can also put 'one' or 'a' in front, but this is very unusual.

These are about <u>one half the cost</u> of adding the additional capacity by using more turbines.

When you are talking about fixed quantities you cannot use the construction with 'of'; you must use 'half' as a predeterminer.

I ordered <u>half a pint</u> of lager.
Can I have <u>half a pound</u> of cooking apples?

You cannot say, for example, 'half of a pint' or 'a half of a pound'.

compound nouns

'Half' can be put in front of many nouns to make a compound noun. Normally in nouns of this kind there is a hyphen.

I gave him a reproachful <u>half-grin</u>.
I first met them in the <u>half-light</u> of an early dawn.
He claimed another goal before <u>half time</u>.

difference between 'half a ...' and 'a half ...'

With many common nouns it is possible to put both 'half a' and 'a half' in front of them. The second alternative sometimes has a hyphen. There is a slight difference in meaning. 'Half a ...' has the idea of an amount which is part of a whole, whereas 'a half ...' suggests an established unit.

I must have had at least <u>half a bottle</u> of wine with the meal.

Uses of 'half'

He had drunk <u>a half bottle</u> of vodka that morning.

In this second example the bottle was a half size.

With time periods and distances such as *hour* and *mile* you typically say 'half an hour' and 'half a mile', but you can also say 'a half-hour' and 'a half-mile', for example if you want to suggest a distinct or precise unit.

He left <u>half an hour</u> ago.
<u>A half-hour</u> later he tried again.
A ticket is £10 for a whole day and £5 for <u>a half day</u>.
The avenue ran straight for <u>half a mile</u>.
The flat they had assigned to me was about <u>half a kilometre</u> away.
The Horse Park is located <u>a half-mile</u> west of Highway 280 on Sand Hill Road.

When there is another determiner or an adjective in front, 'half' is typically used as part of a compound noun (but note there is not always a hyphen).

She dialled his number <u>every half-hour</u>.
<u>Another half-minute</u> would surely have been enough.
He wasn't expecting to enjoy <u>the next half-hour</u>.
They have checkpoints, roadblocks <u>every half mile</u> or so.
Two special ponds were dug for the newts, <u>a safe half-mile</u> away.
Brine realised it would be <u>a full half-hour</u> before Myra would get home.

'half' in times In this last example you could also say 'fully half an hour'.

You use 'half' in times to indicate 30 minutes after an hour. Normally you must say 'half past'.

It was about <u>half past six</u> when she heard Patrick's key in the door.

But in informal English you can leave out 'past'.

I will try and give you a ring about <u>half six</u> tonight.

Chapter 5

as adverb You can also use 'half' as an adverb before verbs and adjectives. The meaning is something like 'partly'.

I half rose then sat back down again.
He half suspected that Paula might try something.
This is surely at least half right.

'Half' can also be a part of compound adjectives.

The Duchess turned away from the half-open window.

meanings as a noun 'Half' has some special meanings as a count noun (with the plural 'halves'). It can mean one of the two parts of a game, in sports such as football, or a half pint of a drink such as beer.

He scored an unusual goal early in the second half.
She sipped a half of lager and listened to his ramblings.

in expressions Someone's **other half** is their husband or wife. This is an informal use.

They said it was high time they met my other half.

To cut, break, or fold something **in half** means into two equal pieces.

I folded it in half.

Not half in informal English can mean 'very'.

It isn't half hard to look at these charts.
They didn't half like it.

This second example means they liked it very much.

It can also be used to emphasize a negative feature.

You're not half the man you think you are.
He hasn't half the strength of character Ritchie has.

To increase or reduce something **by half** means that half of the amount is added or taken away.

Taxes were slashed, bringing top rates down by half.

6 Talking about the existence of an amount or number of something

some, any, no

These are three of the most important words in English so it is important to get them right. You use **some** to talk about a certain number or amount of something, to say or suggest that it exists, but without being precise. You use **any** when you are not sure whether something exists; you will find information in Chapter 7 about another use of 'any'. You use **no** in front of nouns when you want to say that something does not exist.

These words are dealt with in the following sections:

    6.1 Basic meaning of **some**
    6.2 Other uses of **some**
    6.3 Uses of **any**
    6.4 Uses of **no**

6.1 Basic meaning of **some**

The basic meaning of **some** is to give the idea of an amount or number of something, without being precise about it. It is like saying 'a certain amount of' or 'a certain number of'. In this meaning you can use it with count nouns in the plural or with uncount nouns.

He wanted to know if I had some ideas for him.
First ask yourself some questions.
He rose abruptly and slapped some money on the bar.
Let's go up and have some tea.

pronunciation   'Some' has two possible pronunciations: /səm/ when unstressed, which it usually is, and /sʌm/ when stressed or when used on its own (for example, at the end of a sentence). Often when you are reading, it is not possible to know if 'some' is stressed; if it is stressed in speech, the idea is that the speaker is drawing attention to something surprising.

There was <u>some evidence</u> of the possibility of an attack.

as pronoun and quantifier

In addition to its use as a determiner, you can also use 'some' as a pronoun and as a quantifier.

If a client is truly lazy, as <u>some</u> are, counseling will fail. We can look back to understand <u>some of</u> our behaviour.

In these two situations 'some' is pronounced /sʌm/.

When 'some' is a pronoun it is usually referring to something that you can work out from the context. For instance, in the following example, it means 'some ideas'.

If the Government has no specific ideas, perhaps readers of this newspaper would like to offer <u>some</u>.

But sometimes it is not referring back but is referring to people in general.

He returned a global hero, an almost godlike figure for <u>some</u>.

'some' or no determiner

Sometimes there is little difference between a noun with 'some' and one with no determiner. If you say 'Some women were screaming' this is close to saying 'Women were screaming'; the first sentence merely stresses that a number of women were involved, while the second makes clear what kind of people were doing the screaming.

'not all'

'Some' is often opposed in meaning to a more precise determiner like 'all'. In the examples below, 'some' means 'not all', and would normally be stressed in speech.

<u>Some</u> but <u>not all</u> states have licensing requirements.
Yesterday's results provided only <u>some</u> of the answers.

'some...some'
'some...others'

When you want to compare two groups of something, you can use 'some' twice.

Other uses of 'some'

Some of the pieces are built in, some are not.
Some parents did it only once a week, some said they never did.

Another possibility is to use 'some' followed by 'others'.

It is not clear why some storms develop into hurricanes while others do not.
Researchers gave toys to some birds but not others.

'some other' You can put 'some' together with 'other' in front of a noun.

I got the story from Tom and some other people who had worked with him.

'some more' Note too how 'some' is used in front of 'more' to give the idea of an extra amount.

She gave Harold some more sweet potatoes from her plate.
We talked some more.

In other words, she had already given Harold some potatoes, and we had already done some talking.

6.2 Other uses of some

'Some' can be a difficult word to understand, because it is used in other ways with special meanings. These are not as common as the use described above but you need to be aware of them. In all of them 'some' is pronounced as /sʌm/ and in some cases the rule about not using it with singular count nouns is broken.

referring to something vague You can use it to show that something is unknown or unimportant to you. It is usually quite informal.

Some man's voice was talking to him.

Note that in this case it can be used with singular count nouns, as in the example.

You can use it to emphasize that something should exist, even though you do not know exactly what it is.

Chapter 6

There must be <u>some very deep reason</u> for this.
She will have to offer her family <u>some explanation</u>.

Again it is also used with singular count nouns. It is stressed.

with time periods

You can use it with nouns referring to a period of time, such as *time*, *hours*, *days*, and *years*, to mean quite a long period.

He had been ill on and off for <u>some time</u>.
After university she became a schoolteacher for <u>some years</u>.

with numbers

It can mean 'about' or 'approximately' when used in front of numbers.

Indonesia is home to <u>some ten</u> per cent of the world's tropical rain forest.
In 1850 <u>some fifty thousand</u> women worked in such places.

In this case 'some' is an adverb. It has a slightly literary tone.

expressing admiration

It can be used to express admiration, again with singular count nouns.

It was <u>some story</u>.

This use is informal and typically American. It is strongly stressed.

as adverb

It can be used as an adverb, meaning a fairly large amount or to a fairly large extent.

On this evidence they'll have to wait <u>some</u>.

This use is informal and typically American.

'some day'

There is also the expression 'some day', meaning at some unspecified time in the future.

They say they'll stop dieting <u>some day</u>, but not right now.

'Some' is stressed here.

6.3 Uses of **any**

You use **any** when you want to talk about something without asserting that an amount or number of it exists. In this sense it is used with count nouns in the singular and plural as well as with uncount nouns.

I can't see any reason for this.
It is not known if there were any survivors in the crash.
It's not making any money.

Chapter 7 looks at another sense of 'any'.

in non-assertive contexts

'Any' is one of the non-assertive determiners that we discussed in **1.8**. It is typically used in negative sentences, questions, conditional sentences, and after words which have some negative idea like 'never', 'hardly', 'without', or 'prevent'. In these situations there is no claim that something exists (see **1.8** for more detail).

We didn't get any complaints.
Nobody makes any money out of old boats winning races.
Have we got any ideas for that?
Then he moved forward without fear, without any emotion.

However, 'any' can be used in other situations where you want to avoid suggesting that something exists.

You must banish any guilt from your life.
He dismissed any thoughts of his finger preventing him from playing.
Your doctor or surgeon will answer any questions you may have.

Here, there is no assertion that there was any guilt or any thoughts. Because you can avoid claiming that something exists by using 'any', it is often a polite way of mentioning something unpleasant.

WARNING

It is not true to say that 'any' is used in negatives and questions instead of 'some'. The two words have different implications, and so it is quite possible to use both in questions and conditionals.

Chapter 6

Has anybody else shown any interest in this?
Have you brought me some money?
If you have any questions, please write to us.
If you have some extra cash, you can pay more.

The difference is in the expectation. With 'some' you are suggesting the amount or number actually exists; with 'any' there is no such suggestion. For this reason, 'some' tends to be used in offers and requests.

Would you like some wine?
Could we have some coffee please?

'Some', however, is relatively rare with negatives, unless used for emphasis.

It should be for all our children, not just some.

Sometimes after a negative, 'some' has a very different meaning from 'any'.

He didn't like some of the ideas.

This suggests that there were some other ideas that he did like. If you said 'He didn't like any of the ideas', this would mean he liked none of them.

as pronoun or quantifier

'Any' can also be a pronoun and quantifier.

I don't give advice to you because I don't have any.
Technically, I haven't broken any of the rules.

before comparatives

You can also use it as an adverb before *different, more, longer*, and other comparatives.

So is it any different to any other car?
I wasn't enjoying life any more.
Landlords say they will not wait any longer.
It doesn't get any easier.

6.4 Uses of **no**

You use **no** to state that something does not exist. It can be used both with uncount nouns and with count nouns in the plural and singular.

Uses of 'no'

> *There is <u>no evidence</u> that the operation increases the risk of breast cancer.*
> *<u>No details</u> of the peace plan have been given.*
> *She had <u>no pen</u> to write down his address.*
> *You've got <u>no chance</u> of getting the job.*

stronger than 'not any' When compared to 'not any', 'no' has more force; it emphasizes the negative. In the first example above, to say 'There isn't any evidence' would not be as strong. However, at the start of a sentence, it is not possible to use 'not any'; you must use 'no'.

> *<u>No</u> decision will be taken before the autumn.*

in notices Note that 'NO' is very often used when something is forbidden, in particular in notices: 'NO SMOKING', 'NO PARKING'.

'none' 'No' is only used as a determiner; it is not used as a pronoun or quantifier. 'None', on the other hand, can be used in this way (but not as a determiner).

> *There were lots of complaints about the boys, but <u>none</u> about the smoke.*
> *I don't know what's going to happen. <u>None of us</u> do.*

You can use it with a plural verb, as in the example above, but a singular verb is considered more correct by some people.

> *The Republicans have ten candidates, but <u>none looks</u> like a winner.*

'no' before comparatives You can use 'no' as an adverb before *longer*, *more*, other comparatives, and *different*.

> *His best was <u>no longer</u> good enough.*
> *This test takes <u>no more</u> than thirty minutes.*
> *She was <u>no better</u> the next day.*
> *He's <u>no different</u> to the others really.*

'no' in answers Remember that 'no' has another completely different use, as a negative response to questions.

> *'Do you know him?'—'<u>No</u>, I don't.'*

7 Talking about the whole of something

all, every, each, any

When you want to talk about the whole of a group of things you can use **all**, **every**, or **each**; you can also use 'all' to talk about the whole of one thing. These three words have different meanings and are used in different ways. Generally 'all' refers to a group as a whole, while 'every' and 'each' refer to a group that is made up of individual members; however, there are also some differences between 'each' and 'every'. You use **any** (in this sense) to pick out one or more from a group, with the idea 'it doesn't matter which'. There is another meaning of 'any' which is dealt with in Chapter 6.

All Britain's motorways are free at present.
Every street has a bar of some sort.
Each farmer was armed with a rifle.
As a result, serious accidents of any kind went unreported.

These four words are dealt with below in the following sections:

    7.1 Major uses of **all**
    7.2 Other ways of using **all**
    7.3 Expressions with **all**
    7.4 Comparison of **all** and **whole**
    7.5 Uses of **every**
    7.6 Comparison of **every** and **all**
    7.7 Uses of **each**
    7.8 Comparison of **each** and **every**
    7.9 Uses of **any**

7.1 Major uses of **all**

You use **all** to talk about the whole or totality of something. It can be used alone in front of both plural count nouns and uncount nouns to generalize about

Major uses of 'all'

every possible person or thing, either in absolute terms or in a particular context.

The fact is that all dogs bite.
All visitors will have to apply for visas.
I gave up eating all beef when I first heard of BSE.
All information will be held in strictest confidence.

WARNING You do not normally use 'all' with singular count nouns. For example, you cannot say 'All child has a right to education'. There are several exceptions to this; these are discussed in **7.2** below.

as predeterminer You can use 'all' as a predeterminer (see **1.9**) with 'the' to talk about everything in a particular group or situation.

I will fill in all the missing gaps.
All the ironing is done.

You can also use 'all' in front of other definite determiners, such as possessives and demonstratives.

She had worked all her life.
They rejected all that technology for political reasons.
There were small bits of truth in all these suggestions.

as quantifier You can also use 'all' as a quantifier. The meaning is the same.

They should then send you all of the software you need.
All of the activities we tried worked.
All of these armies would have the manpower to fight a long war.

This is more common in American English than British English.

WARNING You cannot use 'all of' in front of a noun without 'the' or another definite determiner. It is wrong to say 'all of people' or 'all of milk'.

before pronouns You can use 'all' as a quantifier before a personal pronoun.

It was an incredible time for all of us.

Chapter 7

You could not say 'for all us' here. But you can use 'all' directly in front of demonstratives when they are pronouns (as well as when they are determiners).

She has ignored <u>all this</u> and made an extra effort.

You can also say 'all of this'.

as pronoun It is unusual to use 'all' on its own as a pronoun, meaning 'everything' or 'everyone'. If you said 'Tell me all', it would sound rather old-fashioned; it would be much more usual to say 'Tell me everything'. However, there are certain situations where it sounds perfectly natural and correct:

- in front of 'about'

I'll tell you <u>all about</u> it later.

- when 'all' is followed by a relative clause (see below)

I'll give you <u>all that I have</u>.

- in fixed expressions referring to things, such as 'if all goes well', 'All is lost', and 'All will be revealed'

<u>If all goes well</u>, the Harlow velodrome could be up and running by next Summer.

- in fixed expressions referring to people, such as 'to all concerned', 'All are welcome', and 'A good time was had by all'.

We hope it will be an enjoyable day <u>for all concerned</u>.

For more expressions using 'all' as a pronoun, see **7.3** below.

Except in the final group of expressions above, 'all' usually refers to things. If you want to talk about people you can say 'all those', followed by a relative clause or other qualifying phrase.

The authorities say they've now released <u>all those</u> detained.

This use is formal.

Major uses of 'all'

with relative clauses

When 'all' is followed by a relative clause it can mean 'everything'.

He accepted <u>all that was good in life</u> as his due.

It can also mean 'the only thing', as in these examples.

It's <u>all I ever wanted to do</u>.
Eventually <u>all I could see</u> was their eyes.

In these two examples the relative clause comes after or before a part of the verb 'be'.

in negatives

It is unusual to use 'all' as part of a subject with a negative verb. This is because a sentence like 'All flats aren't expensive' could have two meanings: 'No flats are expensive', or 'Not all flats are expensive'.

delayed 'all'

Another way to use 'all' is to put it later in the sentence, after the noun it is referring to.

Our muscles and our joints <u>all</u> need regular exercise.

This is the same as saying 'All our muscles and joints'. This pattern is very common with personal pronouns.

They <u>all</u> love flying.
And then <u>we all</u> decided to have false names.

'They all' is the same as saying 'all of them'; 'we all' is the same as 'all of us'.

position of delayed 'all'

You must be careful with the position of this delayed 'all' when it goes with the subject of a sentence. If there is only one verb, 'all' goes in front of it, as in the examples above, but if the verb is 'be', then 'all' goes after it.

We <u>are all</u> flight attendants.

If there are auxiliary verbs, it goes after the first one.

We'<u>d all</u> like to make easy money.
They'<u>re all</u> drinking wine or brandy.

Some people consider that it is not correct to put 'all' before 'be' or an auxiliary verb ('They all are drinking'). However, it does occur in spoken English, particularly American English, when 'all' is stressed.

83

Chapter 7

They all are just interested in making money.

And there is one situation where you must use this word order: when the part of a sentence after the auxiliary verb has been left out to avoid repetition.

He was influenced by his background but we all are.
If one moved, they all would.

delayed 'all' with objects

'All' can also be used in this way with objects that come after the verb, but only with personal pronouns.

Thank you all for your calls.
While we can have it all, we can't do it all.

You cannot say 'I like the people all'.

summary of 'all'

To summarize what has been said so far, you can use 'all' in the following ways:

> *All* lies are bad.
> *All* the lies are bad.
> *All* of the lies are bad
> The lies are *all* bad.
> *All* of them are bad.
> They are *all* bad.
> *All* are bad.
> They *all* are bad.

Of these alternatives, 'All are bad' would be relatively rare, and 'They all are bad' would not be considered correct by some speakers.

7.2 Other ways of using **all**

in time expressions

'All' is commonly used as a determiner with singular count nouns like *day, night, morning, week, month, year,* and the names of seasons to talk about the whole of a period of time.

It took all night to blow up two balloons.
I'll be tied up all day now.
All summer they were excavating the courtyard outside.

These expressions can also be formed with 'the' ('all the night'), and, more rarely, with 'of the' ('all of the

Other ways of using 'all'

night'). There is also the expression 'all the time', meaning 'constantly' or 'regularly'.

I was in a state of panic and anxiety <u>all the time</u>.
He did not tell the truth <u>all the time</u>.

with singular count nouns

There are some other singular count nouns which can be used with 'all'. These are words such as *way, world, family, book, country,* and *house,* which can also be thought of as having parts which together make up a whole.

So I drove <u>all the way</u> down there.
<u>All the world</u> knows.
I'd got <u>all the house</u> done and everything all sorted.

The definite article, 'the', is necessary here. You could also say 'all of the way' and 'all of the world'.

Sometimes a noun which is normally count may be used as an uncount noun to talk about an abstract quality, rather than an object. In this case you can put 'all' in front of it without a definite determiner.

You're <u>all heart</u>.
One was <u>all head</u>, the other <u>all heart</u>.

Here 'heart' has the idea of kindness; the speaker here thinks the other person is very kind.

with abstract nouns

You can use 'all' in front of some abstract uncount nouns after 'in' and 'with', with the meaning 'complete'.

He had to admit, <u>in all honesty</u>, that it was exceptional.
And I say that <u>with all sincerity</u>.

Other words that you can use in this way are *certainty, seriousness,* and *fairness.*

as adverb

'All' can be used as an adverb in a number of different contexts. You can put it in front of prepositions which refer to an amount of space or time, such as *over, through, round, around,* and *along.* It means something like 'everywhere' or 'all the time'.

Oxfam has local offices <u>all over</u> the UK and Ireland.

Chapter 7

> *I have traffic <u>all round</u> me.*
> *She kept quiet <u>all through</u> breakfast.*

You can also use 'all' before certain adjectives and adverbs, such as *alone*, *excited*, and *wrong*. This is an informal, spoken use. There is a similar use with the preposition *about*.

> *She lives <u>all alone</u> in a tiny, dingy apartment.*
> *You make it seem <u>all wrong</u> when it isn't.*
> *My back feels <u>all achy</u>.*
> *Fashion is <u>all about</u> creating an individual style.*

in compound adjectives

You can use 'all' with a noun or adjective to form a compound adjective; when you do this, you usually use a hyphen.

> *She was head girl at her <u>all-girls</u> school.*
> *Morale has slumped to an <u>all-time</u> low.*
> *His <u>all-black</u> outfit matched his mood.*

A number of adjectives and present participles, such as *important*, *pervasive*, *powerful*, *encompassing*, *consuming*, and *embracing*, can be preceded by 'all' (with or without a hyphen). This adds an idea of completeness.

> *The right blend of coffee bean is <u>all important</u>.*
> *The era of the grand ideologies, <u>all encompassing</u>, <u>all pervasive</u>, is over.*
> *He can only do what our <u>all-powerful</u> and <u>all-knowing</u> God allows him to do.*

in scores

You can use 'all' in scores to show that both sides in a game or competition have the same score.

> *The match ended in a <u>two-all</u> draw.*

7.3 Expressions with **all**

All is used in many common expressions. Here are some:

You can use **above all** to show that the last item in a list is more important than the others.

Expressions with 'all'

They are smart, sophisticated, and, <u>above all</u>, have developed excellent menus.

You can use **after all** to show the reason why you said something, or to show a change of opinion.

They began to worry if that might be dangerous. <u>After all</u>, clearly there were armed people about.
Well perhaps, <u>after all</u>, you were right.

You can use **all but** to emphasize that something is (or was) very close to being true.

When she opened his bedroom door the next morning, he <u>all but</u> shouted at her.

You can use **all in all** to give a summary or to generalize.

<u>All in all</u>, this life was not without its charm.

You can use **at all** to emphasize the negative element in a sentence, or with a word which has a negative idea.

I've got no money <u>at all</u> at the moment.
It scarcely mentions women <u>at all</u>.

It is also used in questions and in other non-assertive situations (see **1.8**).

Did you know him <u>at all</u>?

You can use **in all** to mean 'in total'.

<u>In all</u> they played thirty games and scored 101 goals.

You can put **of all** after *first*, *last*, or a superlative for emphasis.

I was met <u>first of all</u> by blank astonishment.
I had endless hours to read and write and, <u>best of all</u>, sit and think.

You can use **that's all** at the end of a sentence to suggest that something does not matter very much.

Chapter 7

Just had a funny dream, that's all.
We picked the wrong guy, that's all.

It can also mean that something is finished.

That's it, that's all for today.

7.4 Comparison of all and whole

When **whole** is used with a definite determiner such as 'the', it has a similar meaning to **all**, but they are used in different ways. 'All' is a determiner and comes at the beginning of a noun group before 'the' and other definite determiners; 'whole' is an adjective and comes after them.

The whole world is one family.

This is the same as saying 'All the world'.

In time expressions

In time expressions the meaning is the same.

We never chatted much during the whole year.

Here you could also say 'all the year'.

You can also use 'whole' as a noun followed by 'of' and a definite noun group.

Use the whole of the foot when walking.

This is like saying 'all of the foot'.

You cannot use 'whole' with uncount nouns; you cannot say 'the whole money' but you can say 'all the money'. One exception is 'the whole time'.

I'm active the whole time.

This is like saying 'all the time'.

'a whole'

You can also use 'a' in front of 'whole', but then the meaning is not the same as 'all'; it is like 'entire'.

The book devotes a whole chapter to the subject.

with plurals

Similarly, with plurals, 'all' and 'whole' (without a determiner) do not mean the same thing. If you say 'All the buildings were destroyed by the earthquake' it

Uses of 'every'

is very different in meaning from 'Whole buildings were destroyed by the earthquake'. The first one means that none of the buildings in question were left standing; the second stresses the fact that entire individual buildings were destroyed.

7.5 Uses of **every**

You use **every** to talk about the whole of a group which has more than two people or things in it. 'Every', more than 'all', gives the idea of a collection of individuals; it is only used with singular count nouns.

It should be compulsory reading for every adult.
I was being pulled in every direction.

WARNING Although 'every' has a plural idea, you must normally use it with singular count nouns. It cannot be used with uncount or plural nouns except in very specific circumstances which are described below.

for separate events 'Every' often has the idea of a series of events happening separately.

On every trip a staff member brings musical instruments.

It would less common to use 'all' here.

If you want to emphasize 'every', you can put 'single' after it.

Government affects every single aspect of our life in this country.

agreement When 'every' is part of the subject, you must use a singular verb form.

Every effort is being made to intensify the blockade.

referring back to 'every' If you want to refer back to a noun group containing 'every' you can use 'it' (or the possessive 'its') if it is clear you are not talking about people, or 'he' ('him', 'his'), 'she' ('her', 'hers') if it is clear you are talking about males or females.

Chapter 7

> *Every newspaper* had the company's name splashed over *its* front page.
> *Every soldier* was sure that *he* was defending *his* own country.
> *Every woman* should try the forbidden at least once in *her* life.

If you are talking about people but it is not clear if they are men or women it is sometimes possible to use 'they', 'them', or 'their' to refer back to a noun group with 'every'.

> Remember that *every person* in your life has *their* own experiences.

Some people do not approve of this use but it is quite common. An alternative is to say 'he or she', but this can be very awkward if it is repeated often.

not as pronoun or quantifier

'Every' is not used as a pronoun or quantifier. You cannot say 'There are so many wonderful places in the world; it is impossible to visit every'; nor can you say 'to visit every of them'.

'every one'

However, you can use 'every one' like a pronoun.

> *He had been in four pubs, and he had bought drinks in every one.*

This means 'in every pub'.

You can also say 'every one' followed by 'of' and a definite noun group.

> *It should be the first boat to win every one of the race's six stages.*

compound pronouns

The three pronouns 'everyone', 'everybody', and 'everything', and the adverb 'everywhere', are related in meaning to 'every'. 'Everything' is used for talking about things, 'everyone' and 'everybody' for talking about people, and 'everywhere' for talking about places.

> *Everyone* must work honestly and conscientiously.
> We want *everybody* to have genuine equality.

Uses of 'every'

Everything was a great deal simpler many years ago.
There was blood everywhere.

'Everyone' is not the same as 'every one'. You can say 'I've read every one of his books', but not 'everyone of his books' because this would refer to people.

repeated time periods and events

'Every' is used very often with words such as *day, year, night, week, morning, hour, minute,* and *month* to talk about repeated time periods.

She was getting better every day.
It attracts around 700,000 visitors every year.

If you want to talk about repeated events occurring at regular intervals, you can put 'every' in front of a number followed by a noun in the plural.

Men think about it, on average, every six minutes.
You will have to attend the clinic regularly every two to four weeks.

You can also use an ordinal number such as 'second' or 'third' after 'every' to indicate the interval involved. For example, if something happens every third week, it happens every three weeks.

These visits had continued regularly, approximately every third week.

In this sense 'every other' means the same as 'every second'.

Departures are every other day from the beginning of August onwards.

'Every' can be added to expressions like 'now and then', 'now and again', or 'once in a while', to emphasize the occasional nature of the events.

Every now and again she kicks me out of bed.
This sort of thing happens every once in a while.

'Every so often' has a similar idea.

They show it every so often on television.

Chapter 7

'every time' You can use 'every time' at the start of a clause to show that one event always goes with another.

Every time you see him he's in a different car.

The meaning is the same as 'whenever'; you can also say 'every time that'.

in proportions You can also use 'every' when talking about proportions. The noun group that follows is plural.

They sell one in every five pairs of shoes in Britain.

You could also express this as a fraction ('one-fifth of all shoes') or a percentage ('20% of all shoes').

'everyday' Apart from the compound pronouns (and adverb) mentioned above, 'every' also appears in 'everyday'. 'Everyday' is not the same as 'every day'; it is an adjective meaning 'common' or 'regular'.

For many people, loneliness is an everyday experience
Formal language has been replaced by the everyday language used in business.

with other determiners 'Every' is often used together with other determiners. You can put a possessive in front of it; 'every' then has an emphatic idea and is rather formal.

Television cameras would be monitoring his every step.

It can also come before 'few', to emphasize a regular occurrence, and 'other'.

Every few days there seemed to be another setback.
Albania is physically cut off from every other country.

Here 'every other' does not mean 'every second', as above; it is like saying 'all other countries'.

with abstract nouns You can use 'every' with certain abstract nouns to express a positive attitude to a statement.

He had every reason to hope for some help from the captain.
I feel I can delegate the task to you with every confidence.

Words that can be used in this way include *chance, confidence, expectation, hope, indication, likelihood, possibility, prospect, reason,* and *right.*

7.6 Comparison of **every** and **all**

similarities 'Every' and 'all' are very similar in meaning; you use both to talk about the whole of something and there are many situations where you could use either (with slight changes). In particular both are used to make generalizations.

Every traveller looks for something different from a guidebook.
All snakes have got teeth.

You could say 'all travellers look' or 'every snake has'.

differences However, there are a number of differences in the way they are used:

- 'Every' is normally only used with singular count nouns; 'all' is used with plural count nouns and uncount nouns, and sometimes singular count nouns.

- 'All' can sometimes be used on its own as a pronoun, 'every' can never be; similarly, 'all' can be a quantifier ('all of the people'), whereas 'every' cannot be.

- 'All' can be followed directly by 'the' and other definite determiners: 'all his ideas'. 'Every' cannot; you cannot say 'every his idea', but you can say 'his every idea'. This is similar in meaning to 'all his ideas' but it is emphatic and formal, and not so common.

- 'Every' and 'all' can both be used before singular count nouns in expressions of time, but the meaning is different. 'Every day' means all the days in question, while 'all day' means the whole of one day.

Chapter 7

7.7 Uses of **each**

You can use **each** to talk about the whole of a group which has two or more people or things in it. It emphasizes the idea that the members of the group are being considered separately.

as determiner You use 'each' as a determiner with singular count nouns.

Children in <u>each class</u> wrote to important people in <u>each country</u>.
<u>Each can</u> is worth just over a penny.

In these examples, although there is more than one class or can involved, you are thinking of them as individual items.

as pronoun and quantifier You can use 'each' as a pronoun on its own.

When two big companies sew up a big deal together they really do it properly. <u>Each</u> has an army of lawyers.

You can also use it as a quantifier.

There were four mounds in a row, <u>each of them</u> about four feet long.

This is very common before a number.

Place a golf ball at <u>each of the ten spots</u> you've marked.
The company has reported declines in profit in <u>each of the past three years</u>.

You must use 'each of' in front of pronouns; for example, you cannot say 'each we' or 'each us'.

<u>Each of us</u> had to care about the other.

'each one' 'Each one' is also common instead of 'each' as a pronoun.

What pictures! <u>Each one</u> was so startling, so special.

with singular verb When 'each' is the subject or part of the subject of a sentence, the verb that follows must also be singular.

<u>Each farmer was</u> armed with a rifle.

Uses of 'each'

referring back to 'each'

When you want to refer back, using a personal pronoun or possessive, to a noun group containing 'each', there are a number of possibilities. If you are talking about something that is not regarded as human, you can use 'it' or 'its'.

Each biography has something different to recommend it.
The survey team maps each river in 500-metre lengths, showing its physical features.

If you are talking about people and the sex is obvious, you can use 'he' ('him', 'his') or 'she' ('her', 'hers').

Each boy gets his wake-up call for school.
Each woman is mistress of her own kitchen.

If the sex is not clear, it is possible to say 'he or she', but this can sound very awkward. Many people prefer to use 'they' ('them', 'their').

Each is aware they have the other person's attention.
Each individual person thinks their case is justified.

in negatives

It is not usual to use 'each' in negatives. Instead of saying 'Each of them didn't do it' you would say 'Neither of them did it' (for two people) or 'None of them did it' (for more than two people).

delayed 'each'

It is also very common to put 'each' later in the sentence, after the noun it refers to.

The sergeants each carried one.

You could also say 'each sergeant' or 'each of the sergeants'.

You can also put 'each' after pronouns.

In fact, we each supplied something the other lacked.

This is like saying 'each of us'.

position of delayed 'each'

With this delayed 'each' you must be careful with the position. If the noun or pronoun is the subject, 'each' is placed in front of the verb, if there is only one, as in the examples above. If the verb is 'be', then 'each'

Chapter 7

goes after it; if there is one or more auxiliary verb, 'each' goes after the first one.

They were each determined to do their own thing.
The big countries would each lose one.

Sometimes you may see 'each' in front of the verb 'be' or an auxiliary.

They each were fitted with a barred door.
The partners each would invest a maximum of $60 million in the new plant.

However, some people do not consider this correct, particularly in written English.

In these cases with a delayed 'each', the noun or pronoun is plural, and if it is the subject, the verb following has plural agreement.

They each face a maximum penalty of two years in jail.

delayed 'each' with objects Delayed 'each' does not occur with a noun or pronoun that is the direct object of a verb. You cannot say 'I know the boys each' or 'I know them each'; you could say 'I know each of them'. However, you can put 'each' after an indirect object, whether it is a noun or pronoun.

Leaphorn gave the boys each a third cigarette.
He handed them each a cup of tea.

after prices and quantities It is very common to put 'each' after prices or quantities, to show that the figure refers to individual items, not the whole group.

The issue price for the shares is $10 each.
They are unlikely to get more than one-third of the vote each.

for repeated events 'Each' is commonly used with time words such as *year*, *week*, and *day*, when you are talking about repeated events.

Get up and go to bed two or three hours earlier each day.

Comparison of 'each' and 'every'

He returned home <u>each year</u> to celebrate New Year with his family.

'Each time' can also be used as a conjunction to say that two things always happen together.

<u>Each time</u> you cut one off, two would grow to take its place.

'each other'   'Each' occurs very frequently as part of 'each other'.

That's why we'll never understand <u>each other</u>.
In some cases these lists contradict <u>each other</u>.

You use 'each other' to say that each member of a group does the same to the others as the others do to them. It is the same as saying 'one another'.

7.8 Comparison of each and every

Each and **every** are similar in meaning, but there are some differences. 'Each' has a stronger idea than 'every' of separate or successive events. But it is also the context, especially the verb, which determines this impression. For example, 'I telephoned every doctor in town' would obviously refer to separate events. You should use 'each' when you want to emphasize this separateness and 'every' when you want to allow for a collective interpretation. For this reason you can use 'not', 'nearly', and 'almost' with 'every', but not with 'each'.

<u>Nearly every</u> person he met wanted something from him.

referring to two   Another difference is that 'each' can refer to two, while 'every' cannot.

<u>Each of the two</u> beach areas has a snack bar.

You could not say 'Every one of the two'. And it would be unusual to use 'every' for other small numbers.

differences in patterns   There are also some differences in the patterns they are used in.

You can use 'each' as a pronoun and as a quantifier; 'every' cannot be used in these ways.

Just tell the students involved that <u>each</u> has a problem to solve.
They walked the streets, <u>each of them</u> penniless.

You could not say 'every has a problem' or 'every of them penniless'. You would have to say 'every one'.

Also, 'each' can be 'delayed', that is, placed after the noun or pronoun it refers to; 'every' cannot. You cannot say 'The boys every bought a present'.

for repeated events Both 'each' and 'every' can be used for repeated events: you can say 'each week' and 'every week'. But with numbers and 'other' only 'every' is possible: 'every second week' (not 'each second week'); 'every two weeks' (not 'each two weeks').

'each and every' There is also the emphatic expression 'each and every', which combines the meaning of both words. Its meaning is similar to that of 'every single' (see **7.5**).

<u>Each and every</u> feature in Victoria Park remains firmly etched in my memory.
It will take strong personal commitment from <u>each and every</u> one of us.

7.9 Uses of **any**

You can use **any** in two different ways. Firstly, 'any' is used to suggest a vague number or quantity of something without stating that it actually exists; it is used in negatives, questions, and other non-assertive situations. You can find out more about this in **6.3**.

in positive sentences The other use of 'any' is in positive sentences where you use it to pick out one or more items from a whole range of things. It has the idea of 'it doesn't matter which'.

The boy's hair was straight and black as <u>any</u> Apache's.

Uses of 'any'

Here the writer is thinking of all Apaches, but wanted to show this by picking out one as a typical example.

You can use 'any' with count nouns in the singular, as in the example above, or in the plural, as well as with uncount nouns.

You've worked as hard as any people I've ever seen.
In Britain, any information is seen as a commodity.

agreement When 'any' is part of the subject of a sentence, the verb following agrees with the noun.

Any friend of hers is an enemy of Eve's.

as quantifier 'Any' is rarely used on its own as a pronoun in this sense. But you can use it as a quantifier.

He said it was 'as important a vote as any of us will ever cast'.

'any one' One way of emphasizing 'any', when it is singular, is to put 'one' after it.

Any one of our employees could be the informer.
Look up D for dentists and pick one, any one.

You should not confuse this with 'anyone'.

You can also put another number after 'any' if you want to make clear the number involved. If you say 'Pick any two from three', it means it does not matter which combination of two out of three is chosen.

You and I are closer than any two people could possibly be.
Buy tickets for any three concerts and get the fourth concert for £5.00.

'just any' If you want to use 'any' after a negative, but still in the sense discussed in this chapter, you can put 'just' in front to make the meaning clear.

It wasn't something I would do with just any woman.
We are not going to sell at just any price.

If you said 'We are not going to sell at any price', it

would probably mean that there is no price at which you are going to sell. By using 'just' you show that 'any' is not part of 'not...any'.

'any other' It is very common to use 'any' together with 'other', especially in comparisons.

It's a disease like __any other__ disease.

8 Talking about a large amount or number of something

much, many

a lot (of), lots (of), plenty (of)

a good deal (of), a great deal (of)

bags (of), heaps (of), loads (of), masses (of), stacks (of), tons (of)

In English there are several ways of talking about a large number or amount of something. The most common words are **much** and **many**; their uses as determiners, quantifiers, and pronouns are described below. Their use with words such as 'so', 'as', 'too', 'very', and 'how' (sometimes called intensifiers) are also described. In addition, 'much' is commonly used as an adverb and is also found in certain common expressions.

There are some restrictions on the way these two words, especially 'much', can be used. These have to do with things like the formality of what you are saying and whether you mean that something actually exists or not. These restrictions are described below in **8.2** and **8.3**.

In addition, there are several, mostly informal ways of talking about large numbers or quantities, such as **a lot** and **plenty**; these are sometimes called *quantifying expressions*. They can often be used instead of 'much' and 'many', and have a particular role in contexts where 'much' and 'many' are not possible. This is especially true of 'a lot of' and 'a lot', which have very few restrictions on their use and are very common in spoken English.

These words are dealt with in the following sections:

    8.1 General uses of **much** and **many**
    8.2 Uses of **much**

Chapter 8

8.3 Uses of **many**
8.4 Adverb uses of **much**
8.5 Intensifiers with **much** and **many**
8.6 Expressions with **much**
8.7 Uses of **more** and **most**
8.8 Other ways of talking about a large amount or number of something

8.1 General uses of **much** and **many**

'much' with uncount nouns

The basic difference between 'much' and 'many' is in the types of nouns they are used with. You use **much** with uncount nouns (see **1.5**) to talk about a large amount of something.

I am delighted that it continues to attract so much attention.
Small investors didn't show much interest in the notes.
He was always tall and later in life put on much weight.

'many' with count nouns

You use **many** with plural count nouns (see **1.5**) to talk about a large number of things or people.

I went to Paris once, many years ago.
Many people have fled their houses in the town.
Many shops in the capital are closed.
She is the author of many books.
There are not many jobs for the men.

as pronouns

'Much' and 'many' can also occur without nouns. You can use 'many' as a pronoun to refer back to a noun already mentioned.

I began looking for a house I could restore. I saw many.

This means 'many houses'. If 'many' is not referring back to something before, then it means 'many people'.

Many have been calling for the postponement of the meeting.

There are restrictions on the use of 'much' as a pronoun and sometimes it is very formal.

The treaty contains much that any socialist would support.

General uses of 'much' and 'many'

See **8.2** for more information.

as quantifiers You can use both 'much' and 'many' as quantifiers (see **1.6**). In this case they pick out a large amount or number of something that has already been mentioned or is known to the listener.

His father attended <u>much of the trial</u>.
<u>Many of the demonstrators</u> came armed with iron bars and hammers.

This is the pattern you must use before personal pronouns.

<u>Many of you</u> have written us to express your thoughts.

with indefinite noun groups You cannot use 'much of' or 'many of' before an indefinite noun group. You cannot say 'many of people' or 'much of money'. However, you can say 'not much of a' before a noun, but in this case there is a special idiomatic meaning (see **8.6**).

vagueness of meaning Both 'much' and 'many' give the impression of a significant quantity or number, but in fact they can be rather vague; the interpretation depends very much on what the speaker and listener expect in a particular situation. In a sentence such as 'Many people left the concert before the end', the actual number could be relatively small (e.g. 50), if that is unusual, or it could be much larger (e.g. 500).

'not much' 'not many' When 'much' and 'many' come after 'not', the meaning is usually the opposite: 'not many' means something like 'few' and 'not much' is similar to 'little'.

I'm looking to see how much canned food I have. <u>Not much</u>.
<u>Not many</u> captains have been replaced after winning a series.

In both of these cases there is a negative idea. However, 'not much' and 'not many' can go with a positive idea; it is possible to say 'He doesn't have much talent, but he does have some'. If this sentence

Chapter 8

were spoken, 'much' would be stressed, as would 'some'.

Sections **8.2** and **8.3** give more details about these two words, including some restrictions on their use.

8.2 Uses of **much**

restrictions on use

Section **8.1** showed that **much** can be used as a determiner ('much trouble'), quantifier ('much of the blame'), and pronoun ('Much depends on this'). However, there are restrictions on the contexts where it can be used. These have to do with two things: whether 'much' is being used in an assertive way (see **1.8** for a fuller explanation) and how formal the style is. Basically, you should be careful if you want to use 'much' in assertive sentences, that is, where you are claiming that something exists; sometimes it is not possible and in other situations it sounds very formal. Generally, however, there is no restriction on using 'much' with intensifiers such as 'so', 'how', and 'too' (see **8.5**).

in non-assertive contexts

There is no restriction on using 'much' as a determiner in non-assertive contexts. These include:

- after negative words like 'not' and 'never':

Even if you tried your hardest it did<u>n't</u> make <u>much</u> difference to the way she treated you.
Even as a young woman she has <u>never</u> needed <u>much</u> sleep.

- with words which have a negative idea:

You can <u>hardly</u> notice <u>much</u> enthusiasm.
Without <u>much</u> surprise Jack recognised his father.

- in questions:

Can they do <u>much</u> damage?

with abstract nouns

In a formal style, 'much' can be used assertively as a determiner, typically with abstract nouns.

Uses of 'much'

There is <u>much confusion</u> concerning the events of October 8th.
The square was the scene of <u>much fighting</u> in last December's revolution.

Here the idea is that the confusion and fighting actually existed.

as quantifier As a quantifier, 'much' is used both assertively and non-assertively, but it is always formal when used assertively.

Hundreds of thousands have been killed, and <u>much of</u> the infrastructure has been destroyed.
He never became rich, having performed <u>much of</u> his work for little pay.
He confesses that he doesn't know <u>much of</u> Parker's music.

As well as with uncount nouns, 'much' can be used with singular count nouns, if they are definite and refer to something which can be divided up.

The man wore sunglasses that concealed <u>much of his face</u>.
The wooden table and floor had absorbed <u>much of the blast</u>.

as pronoun As a pronoun, 'much' can be used assertively as the subject of a sentence in a formal style.

She said the talks had been fruitful, but that <u>much</u> remained to be done.
<u>Much</u> depends on the weather.

As an object, 'much' is very formal when used assertively.

Nationalism has done <u>much</u> to shape our modern world.

'Much' is not used assertively at the end of a sentence. You do not say 'He bought much', or 'She wants much'. Instead you would say 'a lot', 'a good deal', or 'a great deal' (see **8.8**). Also, 'much' is not used in short answers; to a question such as 'How much money does he have?', you cannot reply 'Much'.

Chapter 8

agreement with verbs — 'Much' is followed by a singular verb form when it is the subject of a sentence, or part of the subject.

Too much is familiar.
It can then calculate how much dust is in the atmosphere.
Much of Tony's work involves showing others how they can make their homes look good.

Remember that if 'much' is used as an adverb, or with intensifiers, then the restrictions described above usually do not apply. See **8.4** and **8.5** below for more information.

8.3 Uses of **many**

We saw in **8.1** that **many** is used as a determiner with plural count nouns.

We have concluded many agreements.

formality — For some people the use of 'many' as a determiner with an object sounds formal, and expressions like 'a lot of' (see **8.8**) are preferred.

Later he got many chances to conduct the orchestra.
They have got many things in common.

This is not the case in non-assertive circumstances (see **1.8**).

They hadn't brought many fans.
Did you make many friends there?

And it is not the case when 'many' is part of a subject noun group, though for some people this still sounds slightly formal.

Many parks close at least from sunset to sunrise.

as pronoun — 'Many' as a pronoun is regarded as formal.

Many are holding out for ten times that price.
This well produced video will appeal to many.
The storm damaged more than 60,000 houses, mobile homes and apartment buildings; many remain unfit for habitation.

Uses of 'many'

This does not apply to 'many' in non-assertive contexts.

I get those from America. They're a talking point but I don't sell many.

in short answers
There is some reluctance to use 'many' in short answers. In response to a question like 'How many have you got?' It would be strange to reply 'Many'. You could say 'Lots' or 'A lot'. However, 'Not many' is perfectly possible.

'Are there any factories left at all?'—'Not many.'

as quantifier
When used as a quantifier, 'many' is not particularly formal.

Many of the cooperative farms have been broken up partially.
The FBI is now asking for help in identifying many of the bodies.

with definite determiners
'Many' is often used with other determiners. You can put it after 'the' or other definite determiners; the meaning is something like 'numerous'.

No one can be blamed for the many errors of fact.
Children also may participate in the many activities the resort offers to all guests.
None of her many lovers seemed to want to marry her.

'the many'
It can also be also be used after 'the' but without a noun, meaning 'the majority of people in general'.

It may not be a choice for the many.
It gave power to the few to change the world for the many.

This is a very formal expression, often contrasted with 'the few' (see **9.4**).

'many other' 'many such'
You can put 'many' in front of 'other' and 'such'.

There are many other sick children.
Is this only the last of many such occasions?

It can also come in front of the pronoun 'others'.

These are problems which the countries of southern Africa share with <u>many others</u> in the South.
It was enough that he was still alive when so <u>many others</u> had been less fortunate.

'many a' 'Many' can also occur as a predeterminer in front of 'a' or 'an'. When used in this way, it suggests a number of things or events occurring separately. This is a formal use.

<u>Many a</u> time his legal training solved problems which seemed insoluble.

This suggests a number of separate occasions. 'Many a' is usually regarded as a single determiner because it behaves quite differently from the ordinary use of 'many'; it is followed by a singular count noun and, when it is the subject, by a singular verb.

<u>Many a</u> successful store <u>has</u> paid its rent cheerfully.

after 'be' 'Many' can be used on its own after the verb 'be' with the meaning 'numerous'. This is a formal use.

The reasons for his going on safari were <u>many</u>.

'a good many'
'a great many' You can put 'a good' or 'a great' in front of 'many' for emphasis. (See also 'a good deal' and 'a great deal' in **8.8**.)

<u>A good many</u> of them have cars.
It was <u>a great many</u> years since he had been there.

'many many' An informal way of emphasizing 'many' is to repeat it.

There are <u>many many</u> businesses that would be quite prepared to put up money.

plural verb Note that 'many' is always followed by a plural verb form when it is the subject or part of the subject of a sentence (except in the expression 'many a').

<u>Many people give</u> me money.

Adverb uses of 'much'

8.4 Adverb uses of **much**

Much is very commonly used as an adverb to modify adjectives and other similar expressions. Here it has the meaning of 'greatly', 'to a large extent', or 'by far'. 'Many' is not used in this way.

You can use 'much' as an adverb in the following situations:

with verbs
- with verbs, to strengthen the action or idea they express. This is very common with intensifiers (see **8.5**).

That way it doesn't hurt so much.
He loved me very much.
Who hates me that much?

'Much' can be used on its own without an intensifier, but then there must normally be a negative or other non-assertive word (see **1.8**), as in **8.2**.

It didn't hurt much.
Solving one alone will not help much.
Few worried much about the execution of thousands of dissidents.

You therefore cannot say 'I like them much', but you can say 'I like them very much'.

position with verbs
Usually you put 'much' after the verb, as in all the examples above. However, there are some cases where it is possible to put 'much' before the main verb, and after the subject or first auxiliary verb. In most affirmative sentences, this is a formal use.

This is a trait I much admire in her.
We would much prefer to be given money.
These factors have much affected the building of nuclear plants.

Verbs which can be used in this way are *admire, affect, appreciate, approve of, dislike, enjoy, look forward to, prefer,* and *regret*. All these verbs have to do with feelings or attitudes.

Chapter 8

A few other verbs – *blame, care, like,* and *mind* – can be used like this if they are in the negative.

Kenworthy <u>didn't much care</u> one way or the other what happened to Devereux.
I <u>don't much like</u> the rest of his stuff.
I do <u>not much mind</u> walking the five miles.

With other verbs, 'much' can be used in this position in the affirmative if it follows an intensifier like 'very' or 'pretty'.

I <u>very much believe</u> that honesty is the best policy.
It <u>very much depends</u> on the individual personality.
Men <u>pretty much like</u> the same things.

There are many verbs which can be used in this way. Here is a list of some of them.

admire	disagree	prefer
affect	dislike	reflect
agree	doubt	regret
applaud	enjoy	resent
apply	envy	respect
appreciate	fear	support
approve of	hope	want
assume	know	welcome
bear out	like	wish
depend	look forward to	

When it is used with verbs denoting a regular event, 'much' can have the meaning of 'often'.

He didn't entertain or go out <u>much</u>.

before comparative adjectives

• before comparative adjectives to suggest a greater degree than the comparative already suggests.

And he's clever, <u>much cleverer</u> than people think.
We will be a <u>much better</u> football team next year.

You can also put 'much' in front of 'more' or 'less' to make the difference greater.

The issues involved are <u>much more</u> complicated than that.
He had <u>much more</u> to give.

Adverb uses of 'much'

It is simply much less specific.

'much the' • before 'the' and a superlative or comparative adjective to emphasize a comparison; it gives the idea of 'by far'. This is a formal use.

China would have been much the poorer without Hong Kong.
It is much the best place in Britain to live.

'much like'
'much the same' • before 'the same' and 'like', giving the meaning 'to a great extent'.

Folks are pretty much the same wherever you go.
The music business is much like any other.

Instead of 'much like' you can also say 'very like'.

before past participles • before the past participle of a verb being used as an adjective.

If anyone thought the affair was over, they were very much mistaken.
He was much taken with the poems of T.S. Eliot.
The following information is intended to help you understand this much-discussed topic.

'much too' • in front of 'too' to give it greater emphasis.

Anything else would be much too obvious.

before expressions with prepositions • before expressions beginning with a preposition such as 'in' or 'to'.

Manchester United are a team much in need of a goalscorer.
That story is much to the point.
His team has been acting the same way, much to the annoyance of his rivals.

'Much' is often used on its own before expressions consisting of 'in' followed by an uncount noun (e.g. 'much in need of', 'much in favour'). The following nouns are typically used in this kind of construction: *demand, doubt, evidence, favour, line, need, use, vogue.*

'Much' can also be used in a similar way before expressions consisting of 'to' followed by a noun in a possessive construction (e.g. 'much to the annoyance of', 'much to my embarrassment'). The following nouns are typically used in this way: *anger, delight, disappointment, dismay, disgust, embarrassment, relief.*

When 'much' itself is modified by an intensifier (see **8.5** below), it can be used before a greater range of prepositional phrases.

It is an example of a regime very much in power.
How much at risk is the smoker?
I think they had Wednesday's game too much on their minds.

8.5 Intensifiers with **much** and **many**

Much and **many** are very commonly used after a group of adverbs that are sometimes called *intensifiers* because they strengthen, or intensify, in some way, the meaning of the word that follows; we have already seen examples of them above. They can be used with 'much' and 'many' when they are determiners, quantifiers, and pronouns, and when 'much' is used as an adverb itself. The most frequent intensifiers are:

'so much'
'so many'
- **so**, which suggests that the speaker finds something impressive or remarkable.

She has lost the man who offered her so much.
We had so many letters.

'too much'
'too many'
- **too**, meaning something in an excessive amount or number, with the idea that it is wrong in some way.

They were criticised for drinking too much.

Intensifiers with 'much' and 'many'

Too much of the discussion about education centers around budget deficits.
He believed too many people would make the group ineffective.

'very much'
'very many'

- **very**, which gives the idea of an even larger number or quantity. In assertive contexts, 'very much' is usually only used as an adverb.

They are also affected very much as mothers.
We all very much regret the loss of life.

It is very common in the expression 'Thank you very much' (or 'Thanks very much'). You cannot say 'Thank you much'. If you use 'very much' as a determiner or pronoun, it must be in non-assertive contexts. (See **8.2** above, or **1.8** for more detail.)

Statistics and surveys often don't prove very much at all.
They can't do very much with them.

You could not say 'They can do very much with them'.

'Very many' is not common, but it can be assertive or non-assertive.

It has a pervasive influence in very many countries.
He didn't have very many intimate friends.

'as much'
'as many'

- **as**, meaning you are comparing two equal amounts or numbers. The comparison can be with something already mentioned or something implied.

Whether a site that attracted only 3,000 visitors annually a couple of years ago can cope with as many per day is questionable. (i.e. 3,000 visitors per day)
People aren't watching as much television on Christmas Day because they use their videos. (i.e. as much television as before)

You can make the comparison clearer by repeating 'as' in front of the second item.

We can take as much as our buyer can supply.
Plant as many as you can afford.

Chapter 8

Many teams have match-winners but no team has <u>as many as</u> Australia.

You can also put a noun in between to show what is being compared.

Travelling by ferry allows you to carry <u>as much luggage as</u> you want.
With nearly <u>as many people</u> and <u>as much land as</u> France, Ukraine is certainly big enough.

You can also use 'as much as' or 'as many as' to indicate a surprisingly large amount or number.

The speed can vary by <u>as much as</u> 15 per cent.
The authorities fear <u>as many as</u> fifty thousand people were killed in the earthquake.

You can use a multiplier (see Chapter 5) such as 'half', 'twice', or 'three times' in front of 'as much' or 'as many'.

The Conservatives got <u>twice as many</u> votes as their nearest rivals.

'how much'
'how many'

- **how**, when the amount or number is not specified, for instance after verbs such as *say, tell, find out, guess,* and *know*.

The organisation will not say <u>how many</u> members it claims.
He told her <u>how much</u> he had missed her while he was away.
It is difficult to estimate <u>how much</u> money is involved.

You can also use it to ask about the extent of a quantity or number.

<u>How much</u> was the library fine?
<u>How many</u> hours a week do you spend listening to the radio?

other
intensifiers

Other possible intensifiers that can be used with 'much' and 'many' are **pretty** (only with 'much'), **that**, **this**, and **however**. All are informal, apart from 'however'.

After all, tomorrow will be <u>pretty much</u> like today.

Expressions with 'much'

His task will be made <u>that much</u> simpler if talks are broken off.
<u>However many</u> practice games you play, understanding only comes from competitive games.

8.6 Expressions with **much**

Much is used in many common expressions. Here are some of them:

You can use **much as** (or **as much as**) as a conjunction, with the meaning 'although...very much'.

<u>Much as</u> I regret it, I'll have to cancel our date.

You can also use **much as** in a different way as a conjunction, to mean 'in roughly the same way as'.

She held the pen <u>much as</u> a young child would do.

You can use **much less** to stress that the situation is worse than expected.

The boy didn't have a girlfriend, <u>much less</u> a wife.

You can use **not much of a** before a noun to show that someone has a low opinion of someone or something.

Then he's <u>not much of</u> a partner.
That might <u>not</u> seem like <u>much of</u> an accomplishment.

If you say you are doing **nothing much**, or you are not doing **anything much**, you mean you are doing nothing of importance, nothing worth talking about.

'So what did you do?'—'<u>Nothing much</u>, actually.'

You can use **too much** to mean that someone or something is impossible to handle.

Children were <u>too much</u> for them.

If you say you do not **see** or **hear much of** someone, it means that you see them or hear about them rarely.

I didn't <u>see much of</u> Harry in the last months.

If you say **as much** after a verb such as *say, think, hint,* or *suspect,* you are referring back to an earlier remark or idea.

It struck me how pleased I was to be there. I said <u>as much</u> to my mother.

This means that I said how pleased I was. 'I thought as much' can mean that a later event proves you are right.

He confessed to his wife, who said she <u>had thought as much</u>.

You can use **so much as** after 'if' or 'not' to give a warning to someone not to behave in a certain way.

Not <u>so much as</u> a memo to your secretary.

You can also use **not so much as** to indicate the minimum that should have been done, although it wasn't.

Not one hug, not one kiss, <u>not so much as</u> a handshake!

You can use **so much so that** to say that the consequences of some event are very severe. You put it after a full stop, semi-colon, or comma.

He himself believed in freedom, <u>so much so that</u> he would rather die than live without it.

If you say **so much for** something, it means that the topic is finished. Often there is an idea of sarcasm.

We even hoped they might influence policy towards us. <u>So much for</u> hope.

8.7 Uses of **more** and **most**

'more' with count and uncount nouns

'More' and 'most' are the comparative and superlative forms of 'much' and 'many'. You use **more** as a determiner to talk about a larger than normal quantity of something. It is used with plural count nouns and uncount nouns.

Uses of 'more' and 'most'

More people will try it and buy it.

It can also mean an extra or additional amount.

I regarded it as a chance to gain more experience.

'more' as quantifier and pronoun

You can use 'more' as a quantifier and pronoun.

He will have to take more of the responsibility for things going wrong.
If they think they could earn more in the private sector, let them try it.

after 'some', 'any', 'no'

You can use 'more' after 'some', 'any', and 'no'.

I have made some more cuts.
He was sure that if he drank any more of this good red wine he would fall asleep.
No more eggs have hatched.

'more than'

If you want to say what you are comparing something to, you can use 'more than' or 'more...than'.

More than that would be fatal.
You always have more power than you think.
The strikes began more than two weeks ago.

'much more' 'many more'

When you want to emphasize the difference in a comparison, you can say 'much more' or 'many more'.

They point out that much more could be done.
Sanctions should be given many more months to work.

'even more' 'still more'

When you are comparing something that is already large or numerous with something larger or more numerous, you can emphasize this with 'even' or 'still'.

Longer platforms will make it possible to deal with even more trains.
The world inevitably would suffer still more agony before the military tide was reversed.

Chapter 8

'more' with adjectives

By far the most common use of 'more' is with adjectives and adverbs, to show that something has a greater amount of some quality than normal.

They are <u>more likely</u> to suffer from heart disease.
Perhaps a girl is envious of a <u>more popular</u> classmate.
She gripped his hand even <u>more tightly</u>.

Here 'more' is an adverb.

'more' as adverb

'More' can be used as an adverb on its own.

Maybe we should use them <u>more</u>.
Peter skied and skied some <u>more</u>.

in expressions

'More' is used in a number of expressions.

You can use **what is more** or **what's more** to introduce an extra supporting argument.

His headache and fatigue not only subsided, but, <u>what is more</u>, his craving for alcohol disappeared.
<u>What's more</u>, by rising past 44, the index surpassed its record level.

You can use **more or less** to say something which is almost but not quite true.

He's <u>more or less</u> retired now.

You can say **more than** to say that someone or something has greater value in a particular role than would be normal or expected.

John Cage was far <u>more than</u> a composer.
<u>More than</u> just a calculator, this is a complete personal organisation system.

You can say **no more than** to emphasize how little an amount is.

The pub was <u>no more than</u> half full.

You can also use **more of a** in front of a count noun to identify something that has a quality to a greater or more significant degree.

Uses of 'more' and 'most'

While Deauville is a holiday resort, Trouville is <u>more of a</u> working town.
He is <u>more of an</u> actor than many critics suggest.

'most' with count and uncount nouns

You can use **most** as a determiner with plural count nouns and uncount nouns to talk about the majority of a particular group or amount of something.

You'll just have to be a bit more careful than <u>most people</u>.
In <u>most cases</u>, however, the husband dies first.
At the European Parliament <u>most work</u> is done in committees.

It often follows 'the', with the idea of 'the largest amount', or 'more than anything or anyone else'.

The organisation which, surprisingly, has attracted <u>the most attention</u> has been the JKLF.

You could also say 'most attention' here.

'most' as quantifier and pronoun

You can use 'most' as a quantifier (without 'the') and pronoun.

<u>Most of the rooms</u> were cramped, dark and dank.
<u>Most of those workers</u> have still been unable to find jobs.
Some potatoes have been harvested, <u>most</u> are still in the ground.
<u>Most</u> hardly know what they are protesting about.
He was frustrated more than <u>most</u>.

'most' with adjectives

The most common use of 'most' is before adjectives and adverbs with 'the' to talk about the largest amount of a quality.

<u>The most important</u> ingredient in any slimming diet is willpower.
New resorts open up worldwide, although Spain, Italy, Greece and Switzerland are still <u>the most popular</u>.
The US dollar is <u>the most readily</u> accepted currency on the island.

Chapter 8

'most' as intensifier

'Most' can also be used before an adjective without 'the' with the meaning of 'very' or 'extremely'; this is a formal use.

That was <u>most kind</u> of you.
He has been <u>most explicit</u> about his escape.

'most' as adverb

There are other uses of 'most' where it is an adverb.

What scares me <u>most</u> is that I'm gonna end up not being married.
Inevitably those who suffer <u>the most</u> are the mothers and children.

'most of all'

You can put 'of all' after 'most' for emphasis.

And <u>most</u> important <u>of all</u>, she had faith in him.
What distinguishes Roberts <u>most of all</u> is his timing.

8.8 Other ways of talking about a large amount or number of something

Apart from 'much' and 'many', there are several other words or expressions you can use to talk about a large quantity or number of something. These include:

a lot (of), **lots** (of), **plenty** (of)

a good deal (of), **a great deal** (of)

bags (of), **heaps** (of), **loads** (of), **masses** (of), **stacks** (of), **tons** (of)

These words are not determiners. If they occur before a noun group, they must be followed by 'of'. You cannot say 'a lot people' or 'heaps money'.

'a lot'
'a lot of'

By far the most common of these expressions are **a lot** and **a lot of**. They can be alternatives to 'much' or 'many' in situations where it is not possible to use these words, or where they would sound too formal in meaning. For some people, however, 'a lot' and 'a lot of' are somewhat informal.

I know <u>a lot</u> about her partner
That's <u>a lot of</u> money.
For <u>a lot of</u> kids he's quite enchanting, isn't he.

Other ways of talking about a large amount or number

In these examples it would sound formal, or wrong, to say 'much' or 'many'.

You can use 'a lot of' in front of both uncount nouns and plural count nouns.

We've got a lot of money to spend.
I think a lot of people will be very excited about it.

You can also use it with a definite noun group to talk about a large quantity of something known or already mentioned.

Mel coughed up a lot of the money himself.
A lot of the people now are working on personal recommendation.

You can also do this with a singular count noun if it represents something that can be divided up.

He was a very generous man and gave a lot of his fortune to charity.
A lot of the city's blocked off to traffic.
I know that a lot of the book was fantasy.

'A lot of' is rare with time periods in written English.

I've known him for a lot of years now.

You can use 'a lot' like a pronoun.

There didn't seem to be a lot left.
I think a lot depends on how accurate you are.
People gathered around him and a lot were panicking.

'A lot' can also be an adverb.

He has helped me a lot.
He was away a lot.

'lots of' You can use **lots of** or **plenty of** in an informal style
'plenty of' with uncount nouns and plural count nouns. 'Lots of' has the idea of a larger number or quantity than 'a lot of'.

She'd be pleased that you've got lots of work coming in.
Lots of people complain about tennis nowadays.

Chapter 8

There's <u>plenty of time</u> for conversation.
There are <u>plenty of other things</u> for families with children to do.
<u>Lots of the white settlers</u> were leaving.
There is <u>plenty of the stuff</u> about.

Both 'lots' and 'plenty' can be used as adverbs, but in a very informal style.

She loves him <u>lots</u>.
She talked about it <u>plenty</u>.

'a good deal'
'a great deal'

You can use **a good deal of** or **a great deal of** to indicate a large amount. They are only used with uncount nouns.

It had taken <u>a good deal of careful planning</u>.
The women do <u>a great deal of the work</u>.

'A great deal' suggests a larger amount than 'a good deal'. They can both also be used as adverbial phrases.

That bothers me <u>a great deal</u>.
My younger daughter jokes with me <u>a good deal</u>.

'bags of' and similar expressions

Bags of, heaps of, loads of, masses of, stacks of, and **tons of** are very informal ways of talking about a large number or amount. You can use them with singular count nouns or uncount nouns.

She's lucky, she's got <u>bags of confidence</u>.
They read <u>heaps of newspapers</u>.
We owe you <u>loads of money</u>.
They still believed that <u>masses of things</u> could happen to them.
They have <u>stacks of toys</u> for the kids.
There was <u>tons of material</u> to go through.

Note that these words do have a more specific literal meaning, for example, 'bags of sweets', 'four tons of steel', 'The men carry enormous loads', and so on. Other words can also be used to give the idea of a large quantity or number, for example, **piles of** and **mountains of**.

Other ways of talking about a large amount or number

agreement with verbs

When any of these expressions is part of the subject of a sentence, the verb agrees with the noun, not with the quantifying word.

A lot of people run the risk of being killed.
This is the reason why lots of money is flowing out of this country.
They probably think loads of people have written.

pronoun-like uses

These words can also be used like pronouns.

There's lots we can do.
I made a conscious decision to eat loads.
Masses went to the cinema week after week.
I have tried to pack a good deal into a few words.

9 Talking about a small amount or number of something

little, a little, less, least

few, a few, fewer, fewest

You use these words to talk about small amounts or numbers. You use **little**, **a little**, **less**, and **least** with uncount nouns (though sometimes also with count nouns – see below) to talk about an amount of something. You use **few**, **a few**, **fewer**, and **fewest** with count nouns in the plural to talk about a number of something.

I've experimented with both types and found <u>little</u> difference.
There was also <u>a little</u> money from writing reports for publishers.
There is <u>less</u> atmosphere to absorb the sun's rays.
They know where to look to get the most information with <u>the least</u> effort.
There are <u>few</u> things I enjoy more than walking round an old cemetery.
He was silent for <u>a few</u> seconds.
There have been <u>fewer</u> problems for travellers who chose to fly.
The characters are drawn with <u>the fewest</u> possible words.

'A little' and 'a few' are regarded as single items, not just as combinations of 'little' and 'few' with the indefinite article. The difference in meaning between 'little' and 'a little', and between 'few' and 'a few', is explained below.

These words are like adjectives in a number of ways: they can be modified by adverbs, they can occur after the verb 'be', and they have comparative and superlative forms in 'less' and 'least', and 'fewer' and 'fewest'.

Basic uses of 'little' and 'a little'

These words are dealt with below in the following sections:

   9.1 Basic uses of **little** and **a little**
   9.2 Uses of **less** and **least**
   9.3 Adverb uses of **little, a little, less,** and **least**
   9.4 Uses of **few** and **a few**
   9.5 Uses of **fewer** and **fewest**

9.1 Basic uses of **little** and **a little**

You use **little** and **a little** with uncount nouns to talk about a small amount of something.

There has been <u>little</u> business between the two companies.
Use <u>a little</u> vegetable oil, such as sunflower seed or almond oil.

difference between 'little' and 'a little'

The difference between 'little' and 'a little' is important. 'Little' has a negative idea; it is like saying 'almost no' or 'almost none'.

There is <u>little</u> doubt that he and his accomplices are guilty.

'A little' does not have this negative idea. It is close in meaning to 'some'.

He played <u>a little</u> golf and enjoyed swimming.

as quantifiers and pronouns

You can use both 'little' and 'a little' as quantifiers and pronouns.

<u>Little of the original material</u> remains.
He will have found <u>little</u> to encourage him.
I caught <u>a little of your discussion</u> about British summertime.
Tell me <u>a little</u> about yourself.

formality

'Little' and 'a little', on their own, as determiners, quantifiers, or pronouns, can sound rather formal. When you want to avoid being formal, instead of saying, for example, 'There is little hope' you can say 'There isn't much hope'.

Chapter 9

'only a little' — You can also say 'only a little'.

We have only a little time in which to succeed.

This emphasizes the small amount of time, but there is still a positive attitude; the speaker thinks that success is possible. If you said 'We have little time', the idea would be negative.

after intensifiers — You can put intensifiers such as *so, too, very, how,* and *relatively* in front of 'little'.

There was so little time left at the end of the afternoon.
There was relatively little comment in the press.
She has said very little and given only one interview.

'the little' — You can also put 'the' in front of 'little' when you are talking about something established or familiar.

The little information that we could glean about them was largely contradictory.
She paid them a generous wage for the little they did.

This use has a negative idea; in the last example, the suggestion is that they did almost nothing.

'what little' — You can say 'what little' to mean 'the small amount of' or 'the small amount that'.

And it satisfied what little appetite he had tonight.
Here they are, taking away what little we have.

'as little as' — You can use 'as little as' to indicate a surprisingly small amount.

The process could take as little as two weeks

as adjective — It is important to distinguish the above uses of 'little' and 'a little', meaning 'a small amount of something', from the use of 'little' as an adjective, where it means 'small'. Whether the following noun is count or not can help. If the noun after 'a little' is uncount, then it is being used as a determiner. If the noun is count, then 'little' is an adjective, as in this sentence:

Inside the baby screamed and a little child talked loudly.

Uses of 'less' and 'least'

If a noun after 'little' is uncount, then it is being used as a determiner. If the noun is plural, then 'little' is an adjective, as in this example.

She gave birth to two attractive <u>little boys</u>.

Some nouns can be either count or uncount. In this sentence, 'mystery' could have either meaning, but it probably means 'a small amount of mystery'.

<u>A little mystery</u> is essential in a woman's past.

'a bit'
'a little bit'

Another, more informal way of saying 'a little' is to use **a bit** or **a little bit**.

I speak <u>a bit of</u> French and understand more.
What we're talking about is <u>a little bit of</u> oil.
I've learned <u>a bit</u>, good and bad, from each of the managers I've played under.
He wrote that text, and I only added <u>a little bit</u>.

9.2 Uses of less and least

Less and **least** are the comparative and superlative forms of 'little'. You use 'less' with uncount nouns to talk about a smaller amount or quantity of something.

This can cause tension, tired muscles, weakness and <u>less control</u> of movement.
It makes <u>less noise</u> than a car backfiring.

'less' as quantifier and pronoun

You can also use 'less' as a quantifier and as a pronoun.

We actually spend <u>less of our national income</u> on health than they do in other countries.
Americans will still be paying <u>less</u> for petrol.

'less than'

If you want to say what you are comparing something to, you can use 'less than' or 'less...than'.

People would stop buying it because it delivers <u>less mileage than</u> gasoline.
Half the group felt they spent <u>less than</u> average.
Rural life <u>less than</u> a century ago could be very hard.

Chapter 9

'no less than' If you say 'no less than', it can often be a way of emphasizing that a quantity is large or impressive.

It contributed no less than £745m to the group's £994m of operating profits.

'less' with count nouns In informal English it is quite common to use 'less' with count nouns in the plural, that is, instead of 'fewer'.

I did expect more food and less people.

For some people, though, this is not acceptable. However, 'less than' seems to be acceptable with count nouns when you are talking about numbers.

He is suffering from a form of leukemia that affects less than 70 children a year.

'much less' 'far less' When you want to emphasize the difference in a comparison, you can say 'much less' or 'far less'.

It takes them much less time to get to sleep.
This means we would have far less chance of winning a war.

'even less' 'still less' When you are comparing an amount that is already small with one that is smaller, you can emphasize this with 'even' or 'still'.

She has no feeling for you and even less for your son.
He would have still less time for his law practice.

'less of a' You can say 'less of a' with a singular count noun to identify something that has a quality to a smaller or less significant degree.

In insurance terms, an office-worker is less of a risk than a sportsman.

'less' as preposition A very different use of 'less' is as a preposition, to talk about an amount from which a smaller amount is taken away.

You are credited with $25 less 17.5 per cent per year.

Uses of 'less' and 'least'

'less' with adjectives

By far the most common use of 'less' is with adjectives and adverbs, to show a negative comparison. This is dealt with in **9.3** below.

'least'

You can use 'least' as a determiner with an uncount noun, and as a pronoun, with the meaning 'the smallest amount'. In these uses it usually follows 'the'.

They know where to look to get the most information with the least effort.
The family often knows the least about their kids.

Like 'less', 'least' is also sometimes used with the plural of count nouns, but again this is considered informal or non-standard.

The candidate with the least votes is eliminated.

In this example, it would be considered more correct to say 'the fewest votes'.

'the least of'

If you say 'the least of' followed by a definite noun group, it means the least important of something.

But these were the least of his concerns.
These drugs were the least of my problems.

For the use of 'least' as an adverb see **9.3** below.

'least' in expressions

There are several common expressions containing 'least'.

At least is very common. You can use it to say that there is still something positive in a bad situation, to correct or refine another statement, or with an amount to say that it is the minimum possible.

If that's selfish, then I'm sorry. But at least it's the truth.
There was nothing on the road for at least 100 miles.

You can use **at the very least** to suggest that it might be possible to say something stronger or more definite than the statement you are actually making.

At the very least this suggests your future does not lie in your hands.

You can add **in the least** to a negative word to emphasize it.

The content of her answer wasn't <u>in the least</u> important to him.

You use **not least** to emphasize a particular case or example that your statement applies to.

Washington journalists – <u>not least</u> those at The Times – were horrified.
South Africa attracts many UK emigrants, <u>not least</u> because of its sunshine.

You can use **to say the least** to show that you are making an understatement.

It was a bit uncomfortable, <u>to say the least</u>.

This suggests that it was very uncomfortable.

9.3 Adverb uses of **little**, **a little**, **less**, and **least**

As an adverb, **a little** has the meaning 'slightly' or 'to a small extent'; **little** means 'almost not'.

<small>'a little' and 'little' with comparatives</small>

You can use both 'a little' and 'little' before the comparative form of adjectives and adverbs.

German is <u>a little more useful</u>.
Lili opened her eyes <u>a little wider</u>.
His legs were in <u>little better</u> shape than they had been the year before.

<small>'a little' with adjectives</small>

You can use 'a little' in front of an adjective.

I'm <u>a little confused</u>.
Things were getting <u>a little difficult</u>.

It is unusual to use 'little' in front of adjectives. However, you can put it in front of *different* and some past participles, such as *changed, known, understood,* and *used*.

Officials say the new scheme is <u>little different</u> from the old voluntary scheme.

Adverb uses of 'little', 'a little', 'less', and 'least'

Sales, however, were <u>little changed</u>.
Doctors are keen to highlight this <u>little-known</u> disease.

with verbs 'A little' is frequently used after verbs.

He relaxed <u>a little</u>.
The sight of the place always made him shiver <u>a little</u>.

'Little' is unusual with verbs, and is very formal. With a few verbs such as *know, understand,* and *suspect* it is possible to put 'little' before the verb.

He <u>little knew</u> what he had started.

If you said 'He knew little' this would change the meaning; 'little' would be a pronoun here. With the verbs mentioned above, 'little' can also come at the beginning of the sentence, where it is treated as a negative word and is followed by subject-auxiliary inversion.

<u>Little do they know</u> about her alternative career.

'a bit'
'a little bit' Two more informal ways of saying 'a little' are **a bit** and **a little bit**.

It does affect us <u>a bit</u>.
I think it is <u>a bit</u> better than we expected.
We can perhaps redress the balance <u>a little bit</u>.

'less' with adjectives You use **less** before adjectives and adverbs to form the negative comparative.

If you feel confident you will be <u>less anxious</u>.
It makes their goods dearer, and so <u>less competitive</u>.
Fatty meat cooks <u>less evenly</u>.

The adjective (or adverb) is often followed by 'than' to show what is being compared.

It's <u>less expensive than</u> most pure essential oils.

'least' with adjectives You can use **least** as an adverb before adjectives and other adverbs to compare something to others in a negative way, as the opposite of 'most'. It is usually preceded by 'the'.

This offers <u>the least painful</u> compromise for the human race.

This implies that other compromises are more painful.

'least' with verbs

'Least' is also used with verbs. Some people find this use formal.

The person he most loved was suddenly the person he <u>least</u> wanted to see.
Colds strike when they are <u>least</u> expected.
Those who should worry the most worry <u>the least</u>.

9.4 Uses of **few** and **a few**

You use **few** and **a few** with count nouns in the plural when talking about a small number of things.

<u>Few countries</u> have accepted this claim.
She was silent for <u>a few moments</u>.

difference between 'few' and 'a few'

The difference between 'few' and 'a few' is the same as that between 'little' and 'a little'. You use 'few' when you want to emphasize the negative aspect of a small number; it is like saying 'not many' or 'almost none'. It has the idea of a number which is disappointingly or unexpectedly small.

The book has <u>few</u> new clues to offer.

This is a criticism of the book; the writer thinks the lack of clues is a problem.

'Few' is often used together with 'more' or comparatives to give a positive idea.

<u>Few</u> things give me <u>more</u> pleasure than to receive flowers.
<u>Few</u> scholars are <u>better</u> equipped to explain all this to us than Professor Morton Cohen.

The first example here means something like 'It gives me very great pleasure to receive flowers'.

'A few' does not have a negative idea. It is almost like saying 'some'.

Uses of 'few' and 'a few'

She filled the silence by asking the old man <u>a few</u> questions.

And only 'a few' can be used with time periods.

He was speaking <u>a few hours</u> before talks with the British Prime Minister.

formality 'Few', when used on its own, is generally quite formal. Instead of saying 'There are few people' you can say 'There aren't many people'. 'A few', on the other hand, is not formal, so it is possible to emphasize a small number informally by saying 'only a few'.

There were as yet <u>only a few</u> street lamps.

as quantifier and pronoun You can use both 'few' and 'a few' as quantifiers and pronouns.

But when she emerged with her new face, <u>few of her friends</u> noticed the difference.
Most were eager for war, but <u>few</u> were trained.
He picked up <u>a few of the playing cards</u>.
While <u>a few</u> became richer, many did not.

'few' after 'be' Like 'many' (see **8.3**), 'few' can be used after the verb 'be'. This use is formal.

Car-parks are <u>few</u> and outrageously expensive.

'few' after intensifiers You can modify 'few' with intensifiers such as *so, too, very, extremely, fairly, relatively*, and *how*.

We have <u>so few</u> role models in positions of authority.
Offices have <u>too few</u> telephone lines.
There are <u>very few</u> films of this sort.
They suffered <u>relatively few</u> casualties.
<u>How few</u> of us know how to do that!

'a very few' You can also say 'a very few'.

Only <u>a very few</u> got close to him.

'quite a few' 'a good few' 'some few' If you want to talk about a number which is more than a few, which is in fact quite large, you can use 'quite a few' or 'a good few'.

<u>Quite a few</u> of the girls haven't left the village.

Chapter 9

I plan to go on a good few years yet.

'Some few' has an idea of 'more than a few' (but less than 'quite a few').

Some few have emerged as peculiarly influential.

'the few' You can use 'few' with the definite article 'the' to pick out a small group which is already established or familiar.

*The few survivors staggered bleeding back into camp.
The President met some of the few who survived the massacre.*

'The few' can have a special meaning when it is used as the head of noun group, that is, without a following noun. It means a small set or minority of people, contrasted with 'the many' (see **8.3**). This use is very formal.

House-owning is not the preserve of the few, it's the reasonable expectation of the many.

with 'next', etc You can put words like *next, last, past,* and *first* after 'the' and before 'few', especially with time periods like *minutes, hours, days, weeks, months,* and *years.*

*The government may fall in the next few days.
Over the last few years, prices have fallen sharply.
Within the past few minutes, the President has issued a statement.
For the first few weeks in jail, it was difficult because I was ill.*

with other determiners Other determiners can be combined with 'few', such as 'these', 'those', and 'what'.

*There have been fears expressed that these few people will lead to a flood later on.
The effect of those few days of rioting was far-reaching.
The ten men have packed what few belongings they have.*

'as few as' You can use 'as few as' to talk about a number of things that is surprisingly small.

Uses of 'fewer' and 'fewest'

As few as one in 40,000 passengers becomes seriously ill.

in expressions Some adjectives can come before 'few' to make a special expression such as **select few** and **chosen few**.

He gathered round him a select few whom he knew to be faithful.
It is a case of feast for the chosen few and famine for the rest of us.

9.5 Uses of fewer and fewest

Fewer and **fewest** are the comparative and superlative forms of 'few'. In this sense they are the opposites of 'more' and 'most'. You use 'fewer' with plural count nouns when you want to make a comparison between two things, to say that one is smaller in number.

Every day there are more vendors and fewer customers.

You use 'fewest' with plural count nouns when you want to say that something is small in number compared to everything else. It is usually used with 'the'.

Whoever got the fewest answers right had to make the tea.
Children seem to have the fewest choices in war.

It can also be used without 'the'. There is no difference in meaning.

Mr Major was the candidate with fewest enemies.
Redheads have fewest hairs, usually around 90,000.

You can use 'fewer', 'fewest', and 'the fewest' as quantifiers and pronouns.

as pronouns and quantifiers *They have few qualifications and fewer of the skills demanded by employers.*
More people are wearing seat belts and fewer are drinking and driving.
Gala scored most goals (74 in 30 games) and conceded fewest, a mere 21.
Whoever got the fewest would win.

Chapter 9

formality — Both 'fewer' and 'fewest', like 'few', are fairly formal. Instead of 'fewer' you can say 'not as many', for instance, in the second of the previous four examples 'not as many are drinking and driving'.

'many fewer'
'far fewer' — When you want to emphasize that the decrease in the number of something is great, then you can use 'many fewer' or 'far fewer'.

There are many fewer regulations governing cosmetics.
The prize is far fewer deaths and injuries on the roads.

'even fewer'
'still fewer' — When you have something that is already small in number and want to talk about something smaller, you can show this by using 'even' or 'still'. 'Even' is placed before 'few'; 'still' can come before or after.

Few economists, and even fewer businessmen, believed in recovery.
But now few people came to Syria, still fewer to the Baron.
Not all of them had gone well, and fewer still had gone as planned.

'fewer than' — You can use 'fewer than' (or 'fewer...than') to make a comparison.

The company sold 3,593 homes last year, fewer than expected.
Women are having fewer babies than ever before.
Only businesses employing fewer than 500 people will qualify.

'no fewer than' — If you say 'no fewer than', it can often be a way of emphasizing that a number is large or impressive.

No fewer than six bank robberies were reported within the space of a few hours.

10 Talking about a group of two

both, either, neither

When you want to talk about a group of two, you can use these three words. **Both** means you are talking about 'all' of the group. You use **either** when you want to pick out one of the group but it does not matter which one. You use **neither** to make a negative statement about a group of two.

He needs to convince both groups that he is sincere.
Either company might inject much-needed capital into the business.
Neither suggestion was taken up by the assembly.

In these cases the group is already familiar or established. This use is typical with words where two possibilities are expected, such as with *sides*, *hands*, or *ends*.

Then with both hands pull once.
Independent travellers are welcome to board the cruise ship at either end of its journey.
Neither side appears strong enough to defeat the other.

You can sometimes use 'each' to talk about a group of two; this word is dealt with in section **7.7**.

These words are dealt with in the following sections:

  10.1 Uses of **both**
  10.2 Uses of **either**
  10.3 Uses of **neither**

10.1 Uses of both

You use **both** to talk about the 'whole' or 'totality' of a group of two which is already established or familiar. It is like saying 'all of the two'.

Both men are in powerful political positions already.

Chapter 10

When you say 'both' it is more emphatic than 'the two'.

agreement 'Both' is always followed by a plural noun group and a plural verb if it is part of the subject.

<u>Both units are</u> largely dependent on the parent company.

as determiner and quantifier You can use 'both' in a number of ways without changing the meaning: as a determiner (as above) or as a quantifier.

Cooperation has played a part in <u>both of this century's world wars</u>.
I feel sorry for <u>both of us</u>.

without 'of' It can also be used as a predeterminer (see **1.9**) without 'of'.

<u>Both his parents</u> are still alive.

So you can say 'both men' (most common), 'both the men', and 'both of the men', with no difference in meaning. But 'the both men' and 'both of men' are not possible.

with personal pronouns When placing 'both' before personal pronouns, you must use 'of'.

Do <u>both of you</u> speak Spanish?

You cannot say 'Do both you speak Spanish?'

delayed 'both' You can sometimes put 'both', like 'all' and 'each', after the noun or pronoun it refers to. This use is called ***delayed 'both'***.

I love you <u>both</u>.

If it is the subject, 'both' is placed before the main verb and after the first auxiliary verb (if there is one).

<u>They both</u> welcomed the president's announcement.
<u>They'd both</u> celebrated their twelfth birthdays.

When used with the verb 'be', 'both' comes afterwards.

Uses of 'either'

Liver and eggs <u>are both</u> good sources of natural iron.

It can also be placed after an object if this is a pronoun.

I thank <u>you both</u> very much indeed.

If the object is a noun, then you cannot use delayed 'both'; instead of 'I thanked the men both' you must say 'I thanked both the men' or 'I thanked both of the men'.

in negative sentences — 'Both' is not normal in negative sentences. So instead of 'Both of my parents are not coming' you would say 'Neither of my parents is coming'.

'both...and' — 'Both' is used in one other important way, when it is not a pronoun or determiner. This is as part of the pattern 'both...and' when you want to emphasize a pair of similar things.

<u>Both</u> lead <u>and</u> alcohol are known to increase aggressive behaviour.
The children's names are listed <u>both</u> down the side <u>and</u> across the top.

You can just say 'both' when it is obvious which two similar things are being referred to.

He's just bored or lonely or <u>both</u>.

Here, 'both' means 'bored *and* lonely'.

10.2 Uses of **either**

You use **either** to pick out one possibility from a group of two, meaning it does not matter which. It has the idea of 'any one out of the two'.

If they let <u>either</u> side down, the result could be disastrous.

agreement — As a determiner, it is followed directly by a singular count noun, and, if this is the subject, by a singular verb.

The problem is deeper than <u>either view acknowledges</u>.

Chapter 10

as quantifier You can also use 'either' as a quantifier. If this is the subject there is normally a singular verb.

I want no one in either of these rooms.
Has either of them ever set foot in the other place?

A plural verb is also used sometimes, but this is regarded as non-standard by some people.

I don't suppose either of them are there now.

Before personal pronouns you must use 'of', as in the example above. You cannot say 'either them'.

with negatives You can use 'either' after 'not' or another negative word; this has a less emphatic meaning than 'neither'.

Blame could not be attached to either side.
It's never been tested in combat for either purpose.
That didn't put either of them at their ease.

But you cannot use 'either' at the start of a sentence in this way; you cannot say 'Either side isn't in the wrong'. Instead, you should say 'Neither side is in the wrong'.

meaning 'each' Sometimes 'either' has the meaning of 'each'; that is, both possibilities are included but are considered separately.

I checked the rooms on either side.

as pronoun 'Either' can be used on its own as a pronoun but this use is fairly formal.

The two sides will have to be better and tougher than either has been in the past.

'either way' There is also the expression 'either way', meaning it does not matter which of two possibilities materializes.

You can kill time by having a look around or by simply sitting in the waiting room. Either way, it is a good idea to take something to read.

'either...or' 'Either' is used in two other important ways. You can

Uses of 'neither'

use it as part of the pattern 'either...or' to present two possibilities, only one of which can materialize.

Either we do it or they crush us.
All life is about change – you either adapt or die.

echoing a negative idea

You can also use 'either' at the end of a clause or sentence after a negative, to show a negative idea that echoes another.

'I don't think that's very fair really.'—'No, I don't either.'

10.3 Uses of **neither**

You use **neither** to make a negative statement about a group of two. It is like saying 'none of the two'.

Nowadays, neither side expects an attack from the other.
Neither of the men paid any attention to her.

agreement

As a determiner, it is followed directly by a singular count noun, and if this is the subject, by a singular verb.

Neither accusation is true.
Perhaps neither attack would need to be successful.

as quantifier

You can also use it as a quantifier. If it forms part of the subject, there is normally a singular verb, even when the noun group is plural. A plural verb is sometimes used, but this is regarded as non-standard by some people.

But neither of these illnesses is expected to have any lasting effect.
Neither of these arguments are sustainable.

This is the pattern you must use before personal pronouns.

Neither of them spoke.

You cannot say 'Neither them spoke'.

as pronoun

You can use 'neither' on its own as a pronoun; this use tends to be fairly formal.

Chapter 10

Neither had brought a swimsuit.

Normally you would say 'neither of them'. As a subject pronoun, 'neither' is sometimes followed by a plural verb, but more correctly by a singular verb.

Neither are recommended for infants up to two years.
Neither is eligible for a US visa.

compared to 'not either'

When you use 'neither', it is usually as a subject, because in other places you can use 'not...either' (see above). When you do use 'neither', it is more emphatic.

They have proposed a deficit-cutting plan that contains neither item.

If you said 'that doesn't contain either item', it would have less force.

inversion

If you use 'neither' at the start of a sentence, before the subject, there is inversion of the subject with the first auxiliary verb.

In neither case have the resources been available.

'neither...nor'

'Neither' can be used in two other important ways, when it is not a determiner or a pronoun. You can use it as part of the pattern 'neither...nor' to present two similar negative ideas.

Neither Stella nor Janice would have kept such letters from him.
He could neither confirm nor deny the report.

echoing a negative idea

You can also use 'neither' at the start of a sentence or clause to echo a negative idea. (You can also use 'nor' in this way.)

'I don't even understand the question.'—'Neither do I.'

There is of course inversion between verb and subject. This is similar to saying 'I don't either'.

11 Other determiners and quantifiers

several, enough

such, what

rather, quite

This chapter deals with a number of words which do not fit neatly into any of the other chapters.

11.1 Uses of **several**

only with count nouns

Several has the idea of more than a few, but less than many; it is similar in meaning to 'quite a few'. You often use it when you want to give a positive impression about a quantity which is in fact rather small. It is used only with plural count nouns.

There are now several books on the market.
Energy is present in several different forms.
They've invited me several times to their home.
There are several things puzzling me.

as determiner, quantifier, and pronoun

You can use it as a determiner, quantifier, or pronoun.

He had already had several articles published.
There are new furnishings in several of the rooms.
This will allow a single satellite to do the work of several.

with 'more', 'such', 'other'

You can put 'several' in front of some other determiners, like 'more' and 'such'.

He is expected to remain in hospital for several more days.
Several such hostels remain in use.

with numbers

'Several' is used frequently with 'hundred', 'thousand', and 'million'.

Several hundred coffee machines were bought for an unusually high price.

Chapter 11

When I was a kid I had <u>several thousand</u> from all over the world.

with time periods

It is also common with periods of time.

He had spent <u>several days</u> in Tangier with his mother.
Traffic was halted for <u>several hours</u> on the main coastal highway.
The crimes were committed over <u>several years</u>.

after definite determiners

'Several' can be used after 'the', possessive determiners, and demonstratives. This use is rather formal.

He fumbled with <u>the several</u> locks on his door.
I was a regular tea drinker until I discovered that <u>my several</u> cups a day were worsening my illness.
She had thought about little else <u>these several</u> months.

11.2 Uses of **enough**

with uncount and plural nouns

Enough is a word you use to show that a quantity or number is satisfactory, adequate, or sufficient. It is used with uncount nouns and plural count nouns.

Make sure you have <u>enough money and petrol</u>.
<u>Enough people</u> will believe that to make it true.

as determiner, quantifier, and pronoun

You can use it as a determiner, quantifier, and pronoun.

They did not have <u>enough information</u>.
Mrs Thatcher has survived because she has given <u>enough of the voters</u> <u>enough of what they want</u>.
I never thought one goal would be <u>enough</u>.

Before a personal pronoun you must use 'of'.

We need signatures and we haven't got <u>enough of them</u>.

Often, with 'enough', there is an idea that a limit has been reached, and more would be bad.

You've caused <u>enough grief</u>.

This is a criticism and a warning not to cause more.

Uses of 'enough'

after nouns

It is possible to put 'enough' after its noun but this use is unusual.

There was <u>room enough</u> for them all.

It would be more usual to say 'enough room'.

'enough...to'
'enough...for'

Often it is not stated why something is sufficient or adequate. But if you want to make it clear, you can use a phrase starting with a 'to'-infinitive or 'for'.

I don't think he had <u>enough imagination to</u> appreciate what a narrow escape he had had.
That's <u>enough to</u> give you the flavour.
The submarine carried only <u>enough fuel for</u> a one-way trip.

not with other determiners

'Enough' is not used with other determiners. You cannot say 'my enough money'. If you want to give an indefinite idea you can use 'a' with an adjective such as 'sufficient'.

Is that <u>a sufficient</u> answer, do you think?

'enough of a'

Or you can say 'enough of a' with count nouns to give an indefinite idea. For instance, 'enough of a difference' is like saying 'a sufficient difference' or 'an adequate difference'.

There ought to be <u>enough of a fire</u> left up there.
I'm already taking <u>enough of a risk</u>.
I'm not <u>enough of a historian</u> to know.

This last example means that the person does not have enough of the qualities of a historian.

as adverb

'Enough' is used in other ways. Its most common use is as an adverb modifying adjectives to say that some quality is sufficient. It is placed after the adjective that it modifies.

No one is <u>interested enough</u>, or <u>active enough</u>, to do it.

You could also say 'sufficiently interested' and 'sufficiently active' here.

Chapter 11

It is also used as an adverb after verbs and other adverbs.

She <u>cared enough</u> about them to want to save them.
You've come to my rescue <u>often enough</u>.

WARNING You do not put 'enough' in front of adjectives that it is modifying. You cannot say 'It is enough big'. This is true even when there is a noun following; 'enough' must come after the adjective.

He was <u>a handsome enough</u> child.
They do not make <u>a big enough</u> impact on voters.

But you put 'enough' before an adjective when it is modifying the whole noun group.

If you are eating a balanced diet you should be getting <u>enough essential vitamins</u>.

after sentence adverbs 'Enough' is used after certain adverbs to make a comment on a situation. Words that can be used like this are: *curiously, funnily, interestingly, oddly, strangely,* and *surprisingly*. For instance, 'strangely enough' is like saying 'What was strange was that...'.

<u>Curiously enough</u>, I don't feel so dejected.
<u>Funnily enough</u>, I was suddenly very hungry.
<u>Interestingly enough</u>, China is becoming a major manufacturer of high-tech equipment.

in expressions 'Enough' is used in a number of expressions.

If you say **Enough!** or **That's enough!**, you want to stop someone doing something.

<u>Enough</u>. I'm satisfied she's telling the truth.
<u>That's enough!</u> Stop filming!

If someone **has had enough of** another person or thing, it means they are fed up with them, or they have lost their patience with them.

The Royal Air Force had finally <u>had enough of him</u>.
I have just about <u>had enough of golf</u> this year.

Uses of 'such'

If you said 'I have had enough golf', this would not have the same idea.

If you say that someone **can't get enough** of someone or something, it means they are desperate for more contact, involvement, or information.

She just can't get enough rugby union.
The public couldn't get enough of romantic Lady Franklin.

You can use **fair enough** in spoken English to show that you think that what someone has said is justified, that you agree with them.

'My life's got better and I don't want to risk it.'—'Fair enough.'

You can use **sure enough** to show that some situation or action was expected or predicted.

I looked around and, sure enough, there wasn't a book in sight.

11.3 Uses of **such**

before all nouns

Such is used before singular count nouns, plural count nouns, and uncount nouns.

It had seemed like such a good idea a few months ago.
There is, as always in such matters, a choice of evils.
Such optimism has become strangely out of place.

Note that before singular count nouns it must be used with 'a' or 'an'; 'such' is a predeterminer here.

I wanted to know how he had come to hold such a deeply disturbing opinion.

meaning

The meaning of 'such' is similar to the demonstratives 'this', 'that', 'these', and 'those', but there is an important difference. 'Such' refers to something similar to what is being identified or pointed out; the demonstratives refer to the actual thing. If you say 'We do not use these methods' or 'We do not use those methods', you are talking about the same methods as someone else. But if you say 'We do not use such methods', you mean 'methods *like* these' (or 'methods like those').

as a pronoun 'Such' can be used as a pronoun, but this is formal.

We are scared because we are being watched – <u>such</u> is the atmosphere in Kosovo.

Here, 'such' means 'like this' or 'like that'.

'such...as' You can put 'as' after a noun group with 'such' to state exactly what you are referring to; 'such' introduces a noun with a general meaning.

Do you believe there is <u>such</u> a thing <u>as</u> evil?
What could she want with <u>such</u> a person <u>as</u> you?

You can also put 'such' after the noun and in front of 'as'. In the above examples, you could also say 'a thing such as' or 'a person such as'.

There would never again be a love <u>such as</u> she had felt for Alex.

'Such a love as' would also be possible here.

'such as' in examples 'Such as' can also be used to give examples. There is usually a comma in front.

Some small gains were made, <u>such as</u> the capture of Bourlon Wood.
Foods which are known stimulants should be avoided, <u>such as</u> coffee and chocolate.
Some causes, <u>such as</u> smoking, are known.

Here the meaning is not 'like' or 'similar to', but 'for example'.

for emphasis 'Such' also has an emphatic meaning. If you say 'He's such a coward!', you mean that he's a great coward or very much a coward.

Mother made <u>such a fuss</u> about it.

In this sense, 'such' (or 'such a') can be followed by an adjective.

Uses of 'such'

They all had <u>such rosy</u> cheeks.
That is what has given them <u>such a bad name</u>.

The meaning here is something like 'very'.

'such...that' You can use 'such' before a noun group followed by a 'that'-clause to say that something was the case to a great extent and had certain consequences.

She was in <u>such</u> a hurry <u>that</u> she didn't even want to take anything with her.
This was <u>such</u> good news <u>that</u> I abandoned all my other projects.

'Such' can also be used as a pronoun in this way, but it is formal.

<u>Such</u> is his obsession with secrecy <u>that</u> he insists on using false names.
He thought that the pain was <u>such that</u> he must faint.

after other determiners 'Such' can come after many other determiners, for example 'some', 'any', 'no', 'all', 'many', 'several', and numbers.

We were all invited to have a drink at the Cafe Royal or <u>some such</u> place.
It's absurd to make <u>any such</u> claim.
There was <u>no such</u> thing as bad publicity.
Like <u>all such</u> stories, that is largely a myth.
There had been <u>many such</u> occasions.
You can meet <u>several such</u> people in one day.
Urban planning is <u>one such</u> form of regulation.

'as such' You can use 'as such' after a word in a negative sentence to show it is not being used in a precise sense.

None of them receives a salary <u>as such</u>.

'suchlike' **Suchlike** is similar in meaning to 'such'. It is usually used as a pronoun at the end of a list.

Perhaps politicians, sociologists and <u>suchlike</u> expect this.

It is rarely used as a determiner.

He would never have had any truck with <u>suchlike nonsense</u>.

11.4 Uses of **what**

in exclamations **What** is used in a number of ways as a determiner. Most of these are dealt with in Chapter 4. But there is one more unrelated use: 'what' is used as a way of expressing a strong opinion or reaction, of making an 'exclamation'. Often there is an exclamation mark at the end of the sentence.

<u>What a mess</u> we have made of everything!

This is similar to saying 'We have made such a mess of everything'. Note that 'what' is placed at the beginning of the clause.

before all nouns 'What' is a predeterminer here. You use it before a singular count noun with 'a' or 'an', as above, before a plural count noun, or before an uncount noun.

They suddenly realised <u>what fools</u> they had just made of themselves.
<u>What fun</u> we could have!

without a verb You can use 'what' without a verb.

<u>What a night</u>!
<u>What rage</u>, <u>what betrayal</u> in that woman's face.

with adjectives You can also use 'what' in this way when there is an adjective before the noun which shows the reason for the exclamation.

<u>What amazing animal and bird life</u> we saw!
'<u>What an extraordinary thing</u>!' I cried.
<u>What a wonderful man</u> Frank was.

in expressions Two common expressions with 'what' are **What a shame!** and **What a pity!**, used to express regret or disappointment about something.

Uses of 'rather' and 'quite'

'I'm afraid I have to get back.'—'What a pity!'
What a pity you won't be able to watch the broadcast itself.
What a shame they can't come.

11.5 Uses of **rather** and **quite**

as predeterminers

Rather and **quite** have similar uses and meanings, but there are important differences. They are both commonly used as adverbs (see below), but can be predeterminers in front of 'a' or 'an' and a singular noun group.

I made rather a mess of it.
The warning had come as quite a shock.

They cannot be used in front of plurals or uncount nouns. You cannot say 'I made rather messes out of them'.

meaning of 'rather'

'Rather' gives the idea that someone or something has the quality implied by the noun in a large measure.

It was rather a pity.
You seem in rather a hurry to get rid of me.

The number of nouns that can be used after 'rather' is limited. You cannot say 'He is rather a manager' because 'manager' does not express a quality. You can say 'rather a pity' because 'a pity' means something like 'sad', that is, it has the quality of an adjective.

meaning of 'quite'

'Quite' gives the idea that something is remarkable or impressive.

He makes quite a noise.
It was quite a surprise to find you here.

'Quite' can be used with a greater range of nouns than 'rather', as it expresses a quality in itself, and does not depend so much on the meaning of the noun. It would be unusual to say 'He makes rather a noise' (although 'It was rather a surprise' would be more likely).

Chapter 11

'quite' with adjectives

When there is an adjective in the noun group, 'quite' can usually be interpreted as modifying the adjective.

Normally I'm quite a cool person on the surface.
We were quite close friends.

These mean 'a person who is quite cool' and 'friends who were quite close'. But 'quite' can modify the whole noun group.

This could become quite a social problem.

This means a great or significant social problem. When 'quite' modifies the adjective, it can come after 'a'.

He is a quite well-known theatre director.

But this use is rather informal and confined to spoken English.

'rather' with adjectives

When 'rather' is used with an adjective in the noun group, it always modifies the adjective.

I thought it was rather a good breakfast.

This means the breakfast was rather good. With an adjective it is also possible to put 'rather' after 'a' and in front of the adjective.

Isn't that a rather mad idea?

But the meaning is the same. You could also say 'rather a mad idea'.

as adverbs

The main use of 'quite' and 'rather' is as adverbs to modify adjectives on their own, or other adverbs, or verbs.

He is quite interested in politics.
The reality was rather different.
He was back quite quickly.
I rather like him.
I'd quite like to have them protected.

'quite a few' 'quite a lot'

'Quite' often modifies 'a few' and 'a lot'.

I've done quite a lot of singing.
Quite a few men have attacks of faintness.

Uses of 'rather' and 'quite'

For the meaning of 'quite a few' see **9.4**.

'rather a lot' 'Rather' can modify 'a lot' and 'few'. 'Rather few' has a
'rather few' negative idea, like 'not very many'.

I've <u>rather a lot</u> of work to do.
He had the impression that <u>rather few</u> pages had been turned since he had last seen the book.

Exercises

The numbers in brackets after the exercise number refer to the relevant sections in the text.

In some exercises the examples are shown exactly as they appear in The Bank of English, the database of English texts that has provided the basis for the grammatical analysis in this book. These examples, which are typically incomplete sentences, are called concordance lines.

1 Introduction

There are no exercises based on this chapter, but see the summary exercises at the end.

2 Possessive determiners

Exercise 2A (2.1)

Put 'my' or 'mine' into the sentences below. The first one has been done for you.

1) All of ......*my*...... friends are coming.
2) .... is the one with the blue stripes.
3) I have to confess it's .... own idea.
4) He is a former colleague of ....
5) Here is .... suggestion.

Exercise 2B (2.2)

Look at these sentences which mention body parts. Work out if the possessive determiners can be replaced by 'the' without changing the meaning. Write 'the' in the gap if it is possible; if not, put a line through the gap. The first one has been done for you.

1) I tapped her carefully on <u>her</u> shoulder. ......*the*..........
2) She's suffering from a pain in <u>her</u> knee. ....
3) He put his hands on <u>his</u> head. ....
4) I shook her warmly by <u>her</u> hand. ....
5) They shot him in <u>his</u> leg. ....
6) On <u>his</u> face he painted the flag of his country. ....

Exercises on Chapter 2

Exercise 2C (2.3)

Use the information in brackets at the beginning of these sentences to fill in the gaps with a possessive determiner and noun. The first one has been done for you.

1) (She died.) The news of ......*her death*...... has saddened everyone.
2) (They were defeated.) .... has opened up the race for the championship.
3) (We appeared.) .... surprised everyone.
4) (She is ill.) We have to postpone the talk because of ....
5) (You helped.) Thank you all for ....
6) (He was appointed.) We only found out his true nature after ....
7) (They will arrive.) They are stuck in traffic so .... will be delayed.
8) (You are present.) .... at this meeting is greatly appreciated.

Exercise 2D (2.4)

Put 'own' into the sentences below where necessary; if it is not necessary, put a line through the gap. The first one has been done for you.

1) Find your ..*own*.. friends; stop stealing mine.
2) One of the nicest features of the flat is that it has its .... garden.
3) He crossed his .... legs and refused to move.
4) Although we told everyone we would provide the food, Chris brought his ....
5) I'll bring my sister and you bring your .... brother.
6) You should buy your .... car, instead of using mine all the time.

Exercises

3 Demonstratives

Exercise 3A (3.1, 3.2)

Choose between 'this', 'that', 'these', and 'those'. The first one has been done for you.

1) And ......*that*...... was the last time I ever saw him.
2) We haven't been having much luck .... year.
3) We have received over 100 responses, but of .... most are not favourable.
4) I've a feeling I've seen .... men over there before.
5) .... is what she wrote about her first film: 'I got the idea from a novel by...'
6) Are you still going out with .... awful man?
7) I woke up .... morning with a headache and I've still got it.
8) Johnny! .... isn't a very nice thing to say.
9) We'll never forget .... holiday. We met so many interesting people.
10) The idea in .... exercise is to put either 'this', 'that', 'these', or 'those' into the gaps.

Exercise 3B (3.2)

Say whether the reason for using 'this', 'these', 'that', or 'those' in the sentences below is to do with closeness or distance in *time*, *space*, *text*, or *feeling*. The first one has been done for you.

1) <u>This</u> soup is delicious; I think I'll have some more.
   (closeness in ......*space*........)
2) 'Who are you talking to?'—'It's <u>that</u> brother of yours.'
   (distance in ....)
3) <u>That</u> night he awoke in the middle of a bad dream.
   (distance in ....)
4) <u>That</u> tree has been there for over 100 years. (distance in ....)

156

Exercises on Chapter 3

5) There's <u>this</u> doctor I went to who is absolutely amazing.

   (closeness in ....)

6) The charity received £7,500, but 90% of <u>this</u> was used in expenses.

   (closeness in ....)

7) They say you stole it. What do you say to <u>that</u>?

   (distance in ....)

8) The weather has been terrible <u>these</u> last few days.

   (closeness in ....)

Exercise 3C (3.2)

Insert a noun after 'this' in the sentences below. Choose from the five possible nouns at the top. Each noun is used once. The first one has been done for you.

        claim   idea   theory   belief   problem

1) At the beginning few people believed in relativity, but now this ....*theory*........ is accepted by all.

2) He says he reached the summit, but this .... is not believed.

3) The world is being swamped with rubbish, and if we don't deal with this .... soon, it will be too late.

4) Scientists have long been aware that the world was not flat, but this .... remained widespread for a long time.

5) It was they who first thought of putting milk in plastic cartons. From this seemingly unimportant ...., they earned a fortune.

Exercises

Exercise 3D (3.3)

In the concordance lines below, say whether the word 'that', in the centre of the line, is a demonstrative (determiner or pronoun) or not. Answer 'yes' or 'no'. The first one has been done for you.

1) Saudi government announced **that** oil prices are to be
2) nuclear forces in Europe. In **that** agreement NATO was
3) price rises on European cars **that** began after the US
4) what sets this era apart is **that** Congress has been in
5) raised over $106 million and **that** brings the amount of
6) perhaps then persuade people **that** any improvement would
7) and her left arm was so sore **that** she had to have it in
8) make our job easier. And in **that** case sometimes it's
9) find the gates locked, but **that** did not prevent them

1) ...*no*... 2) .... 3) .... 4) .... 5) .... 6) ....
7) .... 8) .... 9) ....

4 'Wh'-word determiners

Exercise 4A (4.1)

Put 'what' or 'which' into the gaps. The first one has been done for you.

1) ...*Which*... of the boys are you talking about?
2) If he resigned now, ... effect would it have?
3) .... side do you think will win, England or France?
4) I've no idea .... the answer is.
5) She has a pleasant manner, ... makes people feel at ease.
6) .... worries me most is their attitude.
7) We arrived at 12, by .... time the party was over.

Exercise 4B (4.1, 4.2, 4.3, 4.4)

Work out whether 'which' is a pronoun or a determiner in the sentences below. If it is a pronoun, just put a circle around it; if it is a determiner, circle the noun as well. The first one has been done for you.

1) I asked them (which books) they preferred.
2) It's an eating disorder in <u>which</u> people lose their hunger.

Exercises on Chapter 4

3) They've discovered a substance <u>which</u> experts say is the hardest there is.
4) <u>Which</u> films have you seen?
5) There is a debate about <u>which</u> experts are right.
6) Of the two candidates, it was hard to predict <u>which</u> voters would support.

Exercise 4C (4.1, 4.2, 4.3, 4.4)

Use the information in brackets to make a sentence using 'whose'. The first one has been done for you.

1) (It was someone's book.) I don't know ......*whose book it was*...... .
2) (She found someone's book.) ....?
3) (His money had run out.) He was just an unlucky person ....
   ....
4) (Most of their players come from abroad.) They are a team ....
   ....
5) (We believe someone's story.) It depends on ....
   ....
6) (Someone's car damaged yours.) You'll have to prove ....
   ....

Exercise 4D (4.5)

Choose between 'what' and 'whatever', or between 'which' and 'whichever' in the sentences below. Cross out the wrong one. The first one has been done for you.

1) ~~What~~/Whatever you say, I still believe he's innocent.
2) We'll soon know <u>which</u>/<u>whichever</u> person is responsible.
3) I'll be able to answer <u>what</u>/<u>whatever</u> questions come up in the exam.
4) <u>Which</u>/<u>Whichever</u> argument they use, we'll be ready for them.
5) Firstly, you need to be sure about <u>what</u>/<u>whatever</u> information you will need.
6) <u>Which</u>/<u>Whichever</u> of us arrives first should book a table.
7) I like them, <u>what</u>/<u>whatever</u> their religion.

Exercises

5 Numbers and similar determiners

Exercise 5A (5.1, 5.2)

In the concordance lines below, work out whether 'one' is a number (for example, by replacing it with 'two' and making other changes to noun and verb). Answer 'yes' or 'no'. The first one has been done for you.

1) I would import at least **one** small load of furniture. I
2) thus equipped I set off **one** August day, the sun as hot
3) is relatively rare that **one** sees the animals themselves
4) now. However, there was **one** incident that came near to
5) my living as a painter. **One** autumn I was staying with
6) a puppy bouncing around **one** in a frenzy of excited yaps
7) afterwards, saying that **one** of the crew would assist us
8) for a cottage, an empty **one**, miles from anywhere, or at

1) ..*yes*.. 2) .... 3) .... 4) .... 5) .... 6) ....

7) .... 8) ....

Exercise 5B (5.3)

Decide whether 'a' or 'the' should go with these ordinal numbers. The first one has been done for you.

1) Tell me ..*the*.... first thing that comes into your head.

2) There was .... second answer to this question.

3) Three of the pilots landed safely, but .... fourth was killed.

4) I saw two large dogs and then .... third one, even larger, appeared.

5) On .... second day of our holiday we all fell ill.

Exercise 5C (5.4, 5.5, 5.6)

Use the percentage figure at the end of these sentences to make a multiplier or fraction. The first two have been done for you.

1) That was ....*three times*............ the number of people we expected. (300%)

2) Only ....*a/one quarter/fourth*............ of the population is eligible to vote. (25%)

3) You need to cut out about .... of the text. (10%)

Exercises on Chapter 6

4) He's about .... her size. (200%)
5) .... the time you're asleep. (50%)
6) That's .... the amount you said it would cost. (500%)
7) About .... of our money is spent on food. (20%)

Exercise 5D (5.6)

Which of the following sentences with 'half' are correct? Which of the correct sentences mean the same? Write your answers on the lines below.

1) When we arrived, they had drunk half a bottle.
2) When we arrived, they had drunk half of the bottle.
3) When we arrived, they had drunk half the bottle.
4) When we arrived, they had drunk one half-bottle.
5) When we arrived, they had drunk half of bottle.
6) When we arrived, they had drunk one half of the bottle.
7) When we arrived, they had drunk a half of the bottle.
8) When we arrived, they had drunk a half-bottle.
9) When we arrived, they had drunk half bottle.

Write the numbers of the correct sentences here. ....

Now divide the correct sentences into groups according to their meaning.

....

6 Talking about the existence of an amount or number of something

Exercise 6A (6.1)

Decide whether the underlined noun phrases should have 'some' or no determiner; cross out the wrong alternative. The first one has been done for you.

1) <u>People</u>/<s>Some people</s> have inhabited Australia for thousands of years.
2) I would like to ask you <u>questions</u>/<u>some questions</u>.

Exercises

3) <u>Forests</u>/<u>Some forests</u> have been completely destroyed in the last few years.

4) <u>Cars</u>/<u>Some cars</u>, if not most, now run on unleaded petrol.

5) <u>Dogs</u>/<u>Some dogs</u> are the best company for old people.

6) I like <u>milk</u>/<u>some milk</u>, whether it's cold or warm.

Exercise 6B (6.1, 6.2)

Look at the time expressions in the concordance lines below and decide whether 'some' suggests a fairly large quantity or not. If it does, write 'yes' in the space below; if not, write 'no'. The first one has been done for you.

```
1)   see it continuing for some months to come. Unless, that
2)   nothing this morning. Some days I don't have much to do
3)   will not be known for some time because of their habit
4)   will need a doctor at some time. So in any average city
5)   salad appeared to be some days old. There were ten or
```

1) ....*yes*........ 2) .... 3) ....

4) .... 5) ....

Exercise 6C (6.1, 6.2)

Put the sentences below into the correct row according to the pronunciation of 'some'. The first one has been done for you.

/səm/: ....

/sʌm/: .....*1*..

1) They live some forty miles away from here.

2) You'll find some adverts for cars in the local newspaper.

3) I've run out of salt. I was wondering if you could let me have some.

4) We need some new ideas.

5) Some man wants to talk to you.

6) Some of you might not agree with what I am going to say.

Exercises on Chapter 6

Exercise 6D (6.1, 6.3)

Insert 'some' or 'any' into the sentences below. The first one has been done for you.

1) Do you have ..*any*.. idea of how much damage you've done?

2) I'm afraid we haven't got .... milk.

3) You've found .... of the money, haven't you?

4) You can try, but I doubt whether .... of you will succeed.

5) I'll deal with .... problems that arise.

6) Shall we go and get .... lunch?

7) There's hardly .... ice in the fridge.

8) I'm afraid I haven't just lost .... of the money; I've lost it all.

9) He went off without taking .... clothes at all.

Exercise 6E (6.3)

Look at each sentence below. The underlined part represents a possible event or situation. Is the speaker suggesting that it is likely? Answer 'yes' or 'no'. The first one has been done for you.

1) If <u>you have found some money</u>, you should tell the police. ....*yes*........

2) Have <u>they broken any rules</u>? ....

3) Have <u>some of your friends been in here</u>? ....

4) If <u>there is any problem</u>, let me know. ....

5) Would <u>you like some coffee</u>? ....

6) You should inform us about <u>any accidents you have</u>. ....

Exercise 6F (6.4)

Decide whether these sentences need 'no', 'not', or 'none'. The first one has been done for you.

1) I have absolutely ...*no*...... idea.

2) .... of the authors were present.

3) We are accepting .... more applications.

4) The dog got all the meat; the cat got ....

5) I'm .... a fool, you know.

163

Exercises

6) He's a nice boy but he has .... got any friends.

7) .... money was ever found.

7 Talking about the whole of something

Exercise 7A (7.1)

Which of these sentences with 'all' are correct? Write the numbers on the line below.

1) All the money will be useless soon.
2) All money will be useless soon.
3) The money will all be useless soon.
4) All of money will be useless soon.
5) All of the money will be useless soon.
6) The money all will be useless soon.

Which are the correct sentences? ....

And which of the correct sentences has a different meaning from all the others? ....

Exercise 7B (7.1, 7.2)

Insert 'all', 'all the', 'all of', or 'all of the' in the sentences below. In some cases there is more than one possibility. The first one has been done for you.

1) Our friends have ....*all*............ called to thank us.

2) According to most religions, ... violence is wrong.

3) No one can tell you .... answers to life's problems.

4) This is a film for .... family.

5) .... us will remember you.

6) I've worked hard .... my life.

7) We will .... miss you.

8) You had better forget .... this.

9) I've been trying to call you .... day.

10) In .... fairness, you have to admit she's right.

Exercises on Chapter 7

Exercise 7C (7.1)

Work out whether 'all' goes with the noun or pronoun that comes before, or with the one that comes after. Put a circle around the right word. The first one has been done for you.

1) (We) are <u>all</u> heroes now.
2) They hate <u>all</u> snakes.
3) The owners are <u>all</u> members of the club as well.
4) We told him <u>all</u> our plans.
5) We have <u>all</u> sorts of oils for sale.
6) I gave them <u>all</u> money.

Exercise 7D (7.1)

In the sentences below 'all' is followed by a relative clause. Decide whether 'all' means 'the only thing' or 'everything' and write the answer in the space. The first one has been done for you.

1) All we can do is wait and see. *the only thing*
2) All they have to do is turn up and vote. ....
3) Almost all we teach is useful. ....
4) She enjoyed all that was good in life. ....
5) In some circumstances this is all that is required. ....
6) All I could think of was how she died. ....
7) He'll be surprised when I tell him all that has been going on.

   ....

Exercise 7E (7.1, 7.2)

Decide whether 'all' goes with the pronoun before it or with the preposition after it. Circle the word it goes with. The first one has been done for you.

1) I found them <u>all</u> (over) the floor.
2) We were <u>all</u> down the pub.
3) He spilt wine <u>all</u> down my dress.
4) They are <u>all</u> round the corner waiting for you.
5) Put them <u>all</u> on the table.
6) We danced <u>all</u> through the night.

Exercises

Exercise 7F (7.3)

Look at the sentences below and decide whether 'all' is part of an expression. If it is, circle the whole expression; if it is not, just circle 'all'. The first one has been done for you.

1) He got the answers (all) right.
2) After all the fighting, they are taking a rest now.
3) I don't like him at all.
4) Above all, you must be careful.
5) All in all, it wasn't a bad party.
6) She can do what she likes. After all, she is the owner of the place.
7) You can buy newspapers at all kiosks.
8) I owe them $5,000 in all.

Exercise 7G (7.4)

Look at these pairs of sentences with 'all' and 'whole' and decide whether they each mean the same thing. Write 'same' or 'different' in the spaces at the bottom. The first pair has been done for you.

1) a) The whole world is watching.
   b) All the world is watching.

2) a) The trip will last a whole day.
   b) The trip will last all day.

3) a) The party lasted the whole night.
   b) The party lasted all night.

4) a) Did you watch the whole of the film?
   b) Did you watch all the film?

5) a) Whole villages were destroyed to build the motorway.
   b) All the villages were destroyed to build the motorway.

1) *same*   2) ....   3) ....   4) ....   5) ....

Exercises on Chapter 8

Exercise 7H (7.5, 7.6)

Decide whether 'all' or 'every' should go in the gaps below. The first one has been done for you.

1) ..*Every*.... human being has a right to happiness.
2) The policeman took down .... of her details.
3) The teacher criticizes his .... idea.
4) It's so hard to decide; I like them ....
5) .... doctors make mistakes.
6) She's eaten .... one.

Exercise 7I (7.7, 7.8)

Decide whether 'each' or 'every' should go in the gaps below. (Be careful – in some cases both are possible.) The first one has been done for you.

1) He falls in love with almost ..*every*.... woman he meets.
2) They set fire to .... of the huts.
3) They .... need a lot of help.
4) .... day he gets up at five to feed the pigs.
5) .... third marriage ends in divorce.
6) I bought ten cassettes and there was a problem with ....
7) .... one of us knows what needs to be done.
8) .... side thinks it will win the battle.

8 Talking about a large amount or number of something

Exercise 8A (8.1, 8.2, 8.3)

Work out whether the sentences below should have 'much' or 'many'. The first one has been done for you.

1) ..*Much*... of the building was destroyed.
2) .... people would disagree with you there.
3) I saw .... of my old classmates at the reunion.

Exercises

4) We haven't got .... but you're welcome to share it.
5) There is still .... work to be done.
6) He has .... influence with .... politicians.
7) There hasn't been .... news of the hostages.
8) He has some friends but not ....

Exercise 8B (8.1, 8.8)

Use 'much' or 'many' to make a question asking for more precise information. The first one has been done for you.

1) 'She has lots of money.'—'How ......*much*...... ?'
2) 'London has lots of theatres.'—'How .... ?'
3) 'We'll need a lot of time to finish the job?'—'How .... ?'
4) 'We've sold loads of furniture today.'—'How .... ?'
5) 'There are still tons of items unsold.'—'How .... ?'
6) 'Don't worry, there's plenty of food.'—'How .... ?'

Exercise 8C (8.2, 8.3)

Say whether the uses of 'much' and 'many' in the sentences below are formal in style or not. Write 'yes' if they are formal; write 'no' otherwise. The first one has been done for you.

1) We have so <u>many</u> bright young people who can't find jobs.
   ....*no*........

2) This misunderstanding has led to <u>much</u> trouble. ....

3) I haven't seen very <u>many</u> petrol stations since we started.
   ....

4) How <u>much</u> money do I owe you? ....

5) For <u>many</u> his style is too simple. ....

6) I'm afraid there isn't <u>much</u> hope left. ....

7) Is there <u>much</u> point in going on? ....

8) I have seen too <u>many</u> similar cases to be surprised. ....

9) <u>Much</u> depends on the weather on the day. ....

10) <u>Much</u> of her life was spent in hospitals. ....

Exercises on Chapter 9

11) Take as <u>many</u> as you need. ....

12) <u>Many</u> of the supporters were dressed in red. ....

Exercise 8D (8.7)

Decide whether 'more' and 'most' in the sentences below are determiners (modifying the noun) or adverbs (modifying the adjective). The first one has been done for you.

1) We had <u>more</u> good news today. ....*determiner*....

2) They possess some of the <u>most</u> advanced technology in the world.
   ....

3) <u>Most</u> intelligent people realize their limitations. ....

4) We're waiting for <u>more</u> favourable conditions before we buy.
   ....

5) Suddenly we saw even <u>more</u> red flags. ....

6) That's a <u>most</u> interesting theory. ....

9 Talking about a small amount or number of something

Exercise 9A (9.1, 9.3)

What is the writer's attitude in these sentences? Negative or positive? The first one has been done for you.

1) There's little hope of any survivors. ....*negative*....

2) A little constructive criticism never hurt anybody. ....

3) The little he knows is useless. ....

4) The position is little different from what it was last year.
   ....

5) Little is known about their civilization. ....

6) We danced a little and then went home. ....

7) A little of what you like can't do you any harm. ....

Exercises

Exercise 9B (9.1)

In the concordance lines below, say whether 'little' or 'a little' is being used as a determiner (meaning 'a small amount of'), or as an adjective (meaning 'small'). The first one has been done for you.

1) felt that my rather skinny **little** body would benefit by
2) mist-covered mountains. A **little** group of Brent geese
3) was inside it. The oil had **little** effect, and though he
4) Malika called faintly, the **little** wild lonely cry that
5) birds and trying to drip a **little** blood from them into
6) from her bottle, there was **little** life in her. I wept

1) ..._adjective_... 2) .... 3) ....
4) .... 5) .... 6) ....

Exercise 9C (9.1, 9.3)

In the concordance lines below, say whether 'little' or 'a little' is being used as a determiner, a pronoun, or an adverb. The first one has been done for you.

1) devouring the carcass; **a little** later, when the first
2) say her name and play **a little** as a kitten does, and
3) I thought she would have **little** sympathy or tolerance
4) body was at that time **a little** over a foot long, quite
5) feed them at night - **a little** surreptitiously, for it
6) strange creatures. Very **little** survives in legend from

1) ..._adverb_.. 2) .... 3) .... 4) .... 5) ....
6) ....

Exercise 9D (9.1, 9.3, 9.4)

Insert 'a little' or 'a few' in the sentences below. The first one has been done for you.

1) I've still got ..._a little_... water left.

2) .... of the cars were untouched by the fire.

3) Here and there, ...people wandered about the square.

4) .... later, the door opened and he came out.

5) I can let you have .... bit of the money now.

6) .... hours later, we realized we had been robbed.

7) We only know .... about them.

8) .... escaped, but most died in the battle.

Exercises on Chapter 10

Exercise 9E (9.2, 9.5)

Contradict these statements, using 'less' or 'fewer'. The first one has been done for you.

1) 'We've got more food.'—'No, I'm afraid we've got ..*less*... food.'

2) 'There are more people than last time.'—'No, I'd say there are ....'

3) 'We need more information all the time.'—'I disagree. We need .... information.'

4) 'I think there are more students this year than last.'—'Really? I'd say there are ....'

5) 'On holiday I always seem to eat more.'—'Well, you really should eat ....'

10 Talking about a group of two

Exercise 10A (10.1)

Insert 'both' or 'both of' into the sentences below. Sometimes more than one is possible. The first one has been done for you.

1) The rules apply to ...*both/both of*... the games.

2) We are .... studying Japanese.

3) You can have your cake, or you can eat it, but you can't do ....

4) .... these countries have a long history of tolerance.

5) .... women have made successful careers.

6) I hear he hates .... them.

7) In this exercise sometimes .... the possibilities are correct.

Exercises

Exercise 10B (10.1, 10.2)

Insert 'both' or 'either' into the sentences below. The first one has been done for you.

1) If ......*either*...... of them wins it will be a disaster.
2) I'll buy .... toy for you, but not ....
3) I'm afraid we lose .... way.
4) .... of them are too expensive.
5) I am very grateful to .... of you.
6) The audience was not impressed by .... singer.

11 Other determiners and quantifiers

Exercise 11A (11.2)

Put the words in brackets into the gaps in the right order. The first one has been done for you.

1) Are you sure there's ......*enough money*...... ? (enough/money)
2) She .... to give him all her money. (enough/cared)
3) It's .... to escape any police car. (enough/quick)
4) Give me .... and I'll finish the job. (enough/time)
5) Do we have ....? (enough/boxes/red)
6) It was a ...., but it didn't work. (enough/clever/idea)

Exercise 11B (11.3)

Insert 'such' or 'such a' into the gaps. The first one has been done for you.

1) He's ......*such a*...... fool.
2) The trouble with .... furniture is that it breaks too easily.
3) .... problems should be ignored.
4) You should think for a while before making .... difficult decision.
5) It's dangerous to have .... long hair.

Exercises on Chapter 11

Exercise 11C (11.4)

Insert 'what' or 'what a' into these sentences. The first one has been done for you.

1) ......*What*...... fools they are!
2) .... lovely long hair you have.
3) .... day I've had!
4) .... anger we saw in her face!
5) .... beautiful sunset.
6) .... fool did that?

Exercise 11D (11.5)

Work out if you can use 'rather' instead of 'quite' in each of these sentences. Write 'yes' or 'no' in the gap at the end. The first one has been done for you.

1) You have to admit he's <u>quite</u> a speaker. ...*no*...
2) It was <u>quite</u> a shock when we saw them standing at the door. ....
3) That's <u>quite</u> a decision you've got to make. ....
4) I'm afraid they made <u>quite</u> a fuss about it. ....
5) That was <u>quite</u> a party we went to last night. ....
6) They are <u>quite</u> well-known. ....
7) I've had <u>quite</u> a day. ....

Exercises

Summary exercises

These exercises are intended to recapitulate points made in the whole book, and they cover material from all of the chapters.

Exercise 12A

Say whether each of the sentences below sounds formal or not. Write 'yes' if it sounds formal; write 'no' otherwise. The first one has been done for you.

1) <u>Much</u> remains to be done. .... *yes* ....

2) <u>All</u> will be revealed in time. ....

3) <u>Neither</u> had brought any money. ....

4) I haven't seen <u>much</u> of them lately. ....

5) <u>All</u> those who wish to leave should do so now. ....

6) This is a luxury for the <u>few</u>. ....

7) <u>All</u> I can say is 'thank you'. ....

8) I found some of the mistakes but <u>many</u> still remain. ....

Exercise 12B

Cross out the incorrect (plural or singular) verb form. The first one has been done for you.

1) Every student <u>has</u>/<u>have</u> another chance to pass the exam.

2) If either of the children <u>fails</u>/<u>fail</u> the exam, it will be a disaster.

3) Most of the money was recovered, but some <u>is</u>/<u>are</u> still hidden.

4) Of the flats we've seen so far, all <u>is</u>/<u>are</u> too expensive.

5) Each of them <u>was</u>/<u>were</u> allowed to make one mistake.

6) Neither <u>has</u>/<u>have</u> a chance of winning.

7) Any one of them <u>is</u>/<u>are</u> a potential murderer.

8) No answer <u>is</u>/<u>are</u> completely correct.

9) Some <u>wants</u>/<u>want</u> to be rich, others happy.

10) Many a crime <u>is</u>/<u>are</u> committed out of need.

Summary exercises

Exercise 12C

Put the determiners in brackets into the gaps in the right order. Some combinations are not possible; in this case put a line through the gap. The first one has been done for you.

1) She caters to ..._his every_........ wish. (every/his)
2) .... buildings should be destroyed. (all/these)
3) This meal is .... specialty. (a/my)
4) .... families will try to stop us. (both/our)
5) .... time he doesn't know what he's doing. (half/the)
6) Out of .... friends we made, we'll miss Barbara and John the most. (many/the)
7) You must make the most of .... chance. (a/such)
8) We've had .... discussion on this topic. (a/many)
9) .... ideas they've used were in fact all his. (many/the)
10) .... minutes we heard the sound of an aeroplane. (every/few)
11) There have been .... attempts to frighten us. (many/such)
12) Is that .... amount to cover the costs? (an/enough)
13) Over .... months we saw very little of them. (several/these)

Exercise 12D

Decide whether the spaces below should have 'of'. If it is optional, put brackets round it. The first one has been done for you.

1) You can fool some ..._of_.... the people.
2) Many .... the answers were wrong.
3) All .... the speakers were excellent.
4) If enough .... the workers protest, the bosses will have to give in.
5) Both .... the sides played well, but only one could win.
6) There is a fire in each .... the rooms.
7) None .... the applicants has the necessary qualifications.
8) Half .... those eggs you sold me were rotten.

Exercises

Exercise 12E

For each pair of sentences, say whether they have the same or a different meaning. The first pair has been done for you.

1) a) We all agreed that we would meet again.
   b) All of us agreed that we would meet again.

2) a) They each promised to come.
   b) Each of them promised to come.

3) a) The club much appreciates what you have done.
   b) Much of the club appreciates what you have done.

4) a) You both knew what you were getting into.
   b) Both of you knew what you were getting into.

5) a) They half understood the new situation.
   b) Half of them understood the new situation.

1) ......*same*...... 2) .... 3) ....

4) .... 5) ....

Exercise 12F

Put 'all', 'each', or 'both' in the best place in the sentences below. The first one has been done for you.

1) We .... have ......*all*...... been .... thinking about you a lot. (all)

2) I love .... you .... (both)

3) He's ambitious, but we .... are .... (all)

4) He gave .... them .... some sweets .... (each)

5) The boys .... are .... being .... awkward. (both)

Answer Key

Exercise 2A

2) Mine
3) my
4) mine
5) my

Exercise 2B

2) the
3) —
4) the
5) the
6) —

Exercise 2C

2) Their defeat
3) Our appearance
4) her illness
5) your help
6) his appointment
7) their arrival
8) Your presence

Exercise 2D

2) own
3) —
4) own
5) —
6) own

Exercise 3A

2) this
3) these
4) those
5) This
6) that
7) this
8) That
9) that
10) this

Exercise 3B

2) feeling
3) time
4) space
5) feeling
6) text
7) text
8) time

Exercise 3C

2) claim
3) problem
4) belief
5) idea

Exercise 3D

2) yes
3) no
4) no
5) yes
6) no
7) no
8) yes
9) yes

Exercise 4A

2) what
3) Which
4) what
5) which
6) What
7) which

Exercise 4B

2) which
3) which
4) Which films
5) which experts
6) which

Exercise 4C

2) Whose book did she find?
3) whose money had run out
4) most of whose players come from abroad
5) whose story we believe
6) whose car damaged yours

Exercise 4D

The correct alternatives are:
2) which
3) whatever
4) Whichever
5) what
6) Whichever
7) whatever

Exercise 5A

2) no
3) no
4) yes
5) no
6) no
7) yes
8) no

Exercise 5B

2) a
3) the
4) a
5) the

Exercise 5C

3) a tenth OR one tenth
4) twice (OR double)
5) Half OR Half of (OR A half of OR One half of)
6) five times
7) a fifth OR one fifth

Exercise 5D

All except 5 and 9 are correct. The correct sentences can be divided into three different meanings:
a) 2, 3, 6, 7
b) 4, 8
c) 1

Exercise 6A

The correct alternatives are:
2) some questions
3) Some forests
4) Some cars
5) Dogs
6) milk

Exercise 6B

2) certain
3) quite a lot of
4) certain
5) quite a lot of

Exercise 6C

/səm/: 2, 4
/sʌm/: 1, 3, 5, 6

Exercise 6D

2) any
3) some
4) any
5) any
6) some
7) any

Answer Key

8) some
9) any

Exercise 6E

2) no
3) yes
4) no
5) yes
6) no

Exercise 6F

2) None
3) no
4) none
5) not
6) not
7) No

Exercise 7A

All except 4 and 6 are correct. Of the correct sentences, 2 is different in meaning from all the others.

Exercise 7B

2) all
3) all the OR all of the
4) all the OR all of the
5) All of
6) all OR all of
7) all
8) all OR all of
9) all OR all the OR all of the
10) all

Exercise 7C

2) snakes
3) owners
4) plans
5) sorts
6) them

Exercise 7D

2) the only thing
3) everything
4) everything
5) the only thing
6) the only thing
7) everything

Exercise 7E

2) We
3) down
4) They
5) them
6) through

Exercise 7F

2) all
3) at all
4) Above all
5) All in all
6) After all
7) all
8) in all

Exercise 7G

2) different
3) same
4) same
5) different

Exercise 7H

2) all
3) every
4) all
5) All
6) every

Exercise 7I

2) each
3) each
4) Every OR Each
5) Every
6) each
7) Each OR Every
8) Each

Exercise 8A

2) Many
3) many
4) much
5) much
6) much influence, many politicians
7) much
8) many

Exercise 8B

2) many
3) much
4) much
5) many
6) much

Exercise 8C

2) yes
3) no
4) no
5) yes
6) no
7) no
8) no
9) yes
10) yes
11) no
12) no

Exercise 8D

2) adverb
3) determiner
4) adverb
5) determiner
6) adverb

Exercise 9A

2) positive
3) negative
4) negative
5) negative
6) positive
7) positive

Exercise 9B

2) adjective
3) determiner
4) adjective
5) determiner
6) determiner

Exercise 9C

2) adverb
3) determiner
4) adverb
5) adverb
6) pronoun

Exercise 9D

2) A few
3) a few
4) A little
5) a little
6) A few
7) a little
8) A few

Exercise 9E

2) fewer (OR less)
3) less
4) fewer (OR less)
5) less
Note that, in 2 and 4, 'less' would not be acceptable to careful speakers of English.

Exercise 10A

2) both
3) both
4) Both OR Both of
5) Both OR Both of the
6) both of

Answer Key

7) both OR both of

Exercise 10B

2) ...either toy...but not both.
3) either
4) Both
5) both
6) either

Exercise 11A

2) cared enough
3) quick enough
4) enough time (OR time enough)
5) enough red boxes
6) clever enough idea

Exercise 11B

2) such
3) Such
4) such a
5) such

Exercise 11C

2) What
3) What a
4) What
5) What a
6) What

Exercise 11D

2) yes
3) no
4) yes
5) no
6) yes
7) no

Exercise 12A

2) yes
3) yes
4) no
5) yes
6) yes
7) no
8) yes

Exercise 12B

The correct alternatives are:
2) fails OR (informal) fail
3) is
4) are
5) was OR (informal) were
6) has
7) is
8) is
9) want
10) is

Exercise 12C

2) All these
3) —
4) Both our
5) Half the
6) the many
7) such a
8) many a
9) The many
10) Every few
11) many such
12) —
13) these several

Exercise 12D

2) of
3) (of)
4) of
5) (of)
6) of
7) of
8) (of)

Exercise 12E

2) same
3) different
4) same
5) different

Exercise 12F

2) I love you both.
3) ...but we all are.
4) He gave them each some sweets.
5) The boys are both being awkward.

179

Index

Lexical items (words and phrases) discussed in the text are shown in **bold** type. Topics, categories of words, and grammatical terms are shown in ordinary type. References are to pages, not section numbers. Bold type is used to guide the reader to the most important references, where a full discussion of the word, phrase, or topic indicated can be found.

a (an) 9, 14, 16
   in fractions 66–67
   in numbers 56
   with ordinal numbers 64
   a few, see after **few**
   a little, see after **little**
   a lot (of), see **lot**
   see also Articles
about 59, 82, 85–86
above all 86–87
Adjectives, see
   Compound adjectives,
      Demonstrative adjectives,
      Possessive adjectives
Adverbs 13, 18–19, 59
   determiners as 10–11
   in front of **enough** 146
   multipliers as 65–66
a few, see after **few**
after all 87
afternoon 39
again
   every now and again 91
a little, see after **little**
all 6, 7, 13, 16, 18, 23, 35, 57, **80–88**, 149
   as adverb 85–86
   as pronoun 82, 83–84
   compared with **every** 93
   compared with **whole** 88–89
   delayed **all** 83–84
   followed by relative clause 83
   in compound adjectives 86
   in time expressions 84–85
   with adjectives 86
   with prepositions 85–86
   with singular count nouns 85
   all about 82, 86
   all of 81, 82, 84
   all the time 85
   all those 82

alone 86
along 85
an, see **a**
and
   in long numbers 56
   use with **half** 69–70
   both...and 139
another 57, 61
any 6, 11–12, 17, 18, **77–78**, 80, 98–100, 149
   with numbers 57, 99
   any more 78, 117
   any one 99
   just any 99–100
   not any 79
anybody 10
anyone 10
anything 10, 115
anywhere 10
around 59, 85
Articles 4–5, 13, 61–62
   see also **a**, **the**
as
   after multipliers 66
   as few as 134–35
   as little as 126
   as many 113–14
   as much 113–14, 116
   as such 149
   much as 115
   so much as 116
   such as 148
at
   at all 54, 87
   at least 129
   at that 42
   at the very least 129
bags of 122
be
   with **few** 133
   with **many** 108

belief 40
bit
  a bit 127, 131
Body parts 24–25
both 4, 7, 13, 16, 18, 23, 35, 137–39
but
  all but 87
Cardinal numbers **55–60**, 99
  in fractions 66
  with ordinal numbers 64–65
case
  in which case 50
Central determiners 13
chosen few 135
claim 40
Clause, see Noun clauses, Relative clauses
Compound adjectives 64, 66, 86
Compound nouns 70–71
Compound pronouns 9–10
Count nouns 6–7
couple
  a couple 59–60
Dates 65
day 84, 91, 92, 96, 134
  one day 61
  some day 76
  these days 39
deal
  a good/great deal (of) 105, 122, 123
Definite article, see Articles, **the**
Definite determiners 3–4, 13, 56, 61, 63–64, 81, 107, 144
Definite noun groups 8, 88
Delayed determiners 11, 83–84, 95–96, 98, 138–39
Demonstratives 13, 16, **31–44**, 81, 144, 147
  personal pronouns as 43–44
  see also **that**, **this**
Determiners
  combinations of 13–17
  definition of 2–3
  frequency of 1
  noun groups without 5, 74
  with different types of noun 6–7
  see also Central determiners, Definite determiners, Delayed determiners, Indefinite determiners, Possessive determiners, Predeterminers, 'Wh'-word determiners
different 78, 79, 130
double 65
dozen 59–60
each 7, 14, 18, 80, **94–97**
  compared with **every** 97–98
  each and every 98
  each other 97
eighth 63, see also Fractions, Ordinal numbers
either 7, 14, 18, 137, **139–41**, 142
enough 6, 14, 18, **144–47**
even 117, 128, 136
'-ever'-words 53–54
every 7, 9, 14, 15, 16, 18, 57, 80, **89–93**
  compared with **all** 93
  compared with **each** 97–98
  each and every 98
  every one 9, 10, 90, 91
  every other 91
everybody, see **everyone**
everyday 92
everyone 10, 90–91
everything 10, 90–91
everywhere 10, 90–91
extremely 133
fair enough 147
fairly 133
far 128, 136
few 7, 11, 12, 14, 16, 17, 18, 107, 124, **132–35**
  every few 92
  rather few 153
a few 15, 18, 124, **132–35**
  quite a few 133, 152
fewer 17, 18, 124, **135–36**
fewest 18, 124, **135–36**
fifth 63, see also Fractions, Ordinal numbers
first 63, 67, 134
  see also Ordinal numbers
for
  enough...for 145
  for one 62
  for one thing 62

181

one for 62
so much for 116
Formality 9, 12, 82, 102, 104, 105, 106, 107, 108, 109, 120–21, 125, 133, 136
fourth
  as fraction 68
  see also Ordinal numbers
Fractions 14, 16, **66–69**
funnily enough 146
Genitive **'s** 23–24, 28, 29
Gerunds
  with possessive determiners 23
get
  can't get enough 147
good
  a good deal (of) 105, 122, 123
  a good few 133–34
  a good many 108
great
  a great deal (of) 105, 122
  a great many 108
half 16, 23, 35, **69–72**, 114
have
  have had enough of 146–47
heaps (of) 120, 122
hear
  hear much of 115
her 18, 21
  see also Possessive determiners
here 36
hers 21
  see also Possessive pronouns
his 18, 21, 22, see also Possessive determiners, Possessive pronouns
hold
  hold your own 29
hour 71
how
  how few 133
  how many 114
  how much 114
however 114–15
hundred 56, 143
Hyphenation 56, 66–67, 70, 71, 86
idea 40
in 85, 111–12
  all in all 87
  in all 87
  in half 72
  in the least 130
Indefinite article
  expressed by **one** 61–62
  see also **a**, Articles
Indefinite determiners 3–4, 57, 69
Indefinite noun groups 67, 103
Indirect questions 49, 52
Intensifiers **112–15**, 126, 133
it
  with noun clauses 52
  that's it 42
it's 22
its 18, 21
  as pronoun 22
  see also Possessive determiners
just any 99–100
kind (noun) 43, 48
last 64, 87, 134
least 7, 12, 18, 124, 127, **129–30**
  as adverb 131–32
less 7, 17, 18, 124, **127–29**
  as adverb 10, 11, 129, 131
  as preposition 128
  less than 59, 127–28
  more or less 118
  much less 110–11, 115, 128
like
  much like 111
little 7, 14, 16, 18, 124, **125–27**
  as adjective 126–27
  as adverb 130–31
a little 7, 15, 18, 124, **125–27**
  as adverb 130–31
  a little bit 127
loads (of) 122, 123
longer
  any longer 78
  no longer 79
lot
  a lot (of) 101, 105, 106, **120–21**, 123
  lots (of) 121–22, 123
  quite a lot (of) 152
  rather a lot (of) 153
make
  make something your own 29
many 7, 11, 12, 14, 15, 16, 17, 18, 51, **101–3**, **106–8**, 117, 133, 136, 149

many (continued)
  after **be** 108
  with intensifiers 112–14
  a good/great many 108
  many a 14, 15, 16, **108**
  many many 108
  not many 103, 107
  the many 107
masses (of) 122, 123
mile 71
million 56, 143
mine 21, 22
  see also Possessive pronouns
more 6, 11, 17, 18, 110, **116–19**, 143
  any more 78, 117
  more than 59, 117, 118
  no more 79, 117
  some more 75, 117
morning 38–39
most 6, 18, 51, 116, **119–20**
mountains of 122
much 7, 11–12, 17, 18, **101–6**, 109–16
  as adverb 109–12
  restrictions on use 102, 104
  with intensifiers 112–14
  with prepositional phrases 111–12
  with verbs 109–10, 111
  anything much 115
  as much 113–14, 116
  hear/see much of 115
  much as 115
  much less 110–11, 115, 128
  much like 111
  much more 110, 117
  much the same 111
  much too 111
  not much 103–4, 115
  nothing much 115
  so much 112, 116
  too much 112–13, 115
Multipliers 13, 16, **65–66**, 114
my 18, 21
  see also Possessive determiners
nearly 59, 97
neither 7, 14–15, 18, 137, **141–42**
never 104
next 64, 134

night 84–85
ninth 63, see also Fractions, Ordinal numbers
no 6, 9, 17, 18, **78–79**, 149
  no fewer than 136
  no less than 128
  no more 79, 117
  no more than 118
  no one 10
nobody 10
Nominal clauses, see Noun clauses
Non-assertive contexts 11–12, 77, 87, 104–5, 106, 109, 113
none 9, 19, 79
no-one 10
nor 142
not 104
  not...either 142
  not half 72
  not least 130
  not many 103, 107
  not much 103–4, 115
  not so much as 116
nothing 10, 115
Nouns, see Compound nouns, Count nouns, Uncount nouns
Noun clauses 51–52, 53
Noun groups 9, 20, see also Definite noun groups, Indefinite noun groups
now 38
  every now and again/then 91
nowhere 10
Numbers 14, 16, **55–65**, see also Cardinal numbers, Ordinal numbers
of
  in front of possessive pronouns 22–23
  with quantifiers 7–8
  all of 81, 82, 84
  of all 87, 120
  that of 33
  those of 33, 34
often
  every so often 91
on
  on your own 29

once
  every once in a while 91
one 10, 34–35, **60–62**
  as part of other numbers 56
  any one 99
  each one 94
  every one 9, 10, 90, 91
  one or two 59
  which one(s) 46–47
ones, see **one**
only 59, 126, 133
or
  in approximate numbers 59
  either...or 140–41
  or whatever 54
Ordinal numbers **63–65**, 91
  in fractions 66
other 57–58, 91, 92, 100, 107–8
  each other 97
  every other 91
  one...other 61
  other half 72
our 18, 21
  see also Possessive determiners
ours 21, 22
  see also Possessive pronouns
over 59, 85
own 28–30
Parts of the body, see Body parts
past 134
  in times 68, 71
Periods of time, see Time periods
Personal pronouns 21, 81–82, 83, 138–39, 140
piles of 122
pity
  what a pity 150–51
plenty (of) 12, 101, 121–22
Possessive adjectives 20
Possessive determiners 6, 13, 16, **20–30**, 81, 92, 144
  with nouns derived from verbs 26–27
Possessive pronouns 9, 18–19, 21, 22–23
Postdeterminers 14
Predeterminers **8**, 13, 14, 65, 67, 70–71, 81, 138, 151–52
pretty 114
problem 40

Pronouns 18–19, see also Compound pronouns, Personal pronouns, Possessive pronouns, Relative pronouns
Quantifiers 1, **7–8**, 18–19
quarter 68–69, see also Fractions
Questions 49, 104
  use of **some** and **any** in 77–78
  see also Indirect questions
quite 11, 14, 16, 18, **151–53**
  quite a few 133, 152
rather 11, 14, 16, 18, **151–53**
Relative clauses 49–51
  after **all** 83
Relative pronouns 43
relatively 126, 133
round 85–86
same 11
say
  to say the least 130
score 59–60
second 63
  see also Ordinal numbers
see much of 115
select few 135
Sentential relatives 50
several 7, 14, 16, 18, **143–44**, 149
shame
  what a shame 150–51
so
  so few 133
  so little 126
  so many 112
  so much 112, 116
  so that 43
some 6, 17, 19, 51, 57, **73–76**, 149
  with negatives 78
  some few 134
  some more 75, 117
somebody, someone 10
something 10
somewhere 10
sort 43, 48
stacks (of) 122
still 117, 128, 136
such 14, 15, 16, 19, 43, 107, 143, **147–50**
suchlike 149–50
sure enough 147

Telephone
  speaking on the 33
Text
  this and **that** in relation to 39–40
than
  fewer than 136
  less than 59, 127–28
  more than 59, 117, 118
thank you very much 113
that 7, 19, **31–43**
  as conjunction 43
  as intensifier 41–42, 114–15
  as relative pronoun 43, 51
  difference between **this** and **that** 35–41
  expressing negative emotion 41
  non-demonstrative uses 33, 34
  on the telephone 33
  referring to person 33
  with **kind** and **sort** 43
  so much so that 116
  so that 43
  such...that 149
  that of 33
  that's all 87–88
  that's enough 146
  that's that 42
  that which 34
  see also Demonstratives
the 4–5, 9, 13
  with body parts 24–25
  much the 111
  the few 107, 134
  the little 126
  the many 107
  the one(s) 60–61
  see also Articles
their 19, 21, 90, 95
  see also Possessive determiners
theirs 21, 22
  see also Possessive pronouns
them
  as non-standard demonstrative 16, 37, 44
then 38
  every now and then 91
theory 40
there 36
these 7, 19, 134

  these days 39
  see also Demonstratives, **this**
thing
  for one thing 62
third 63, 67, see also Fractions, Ordinal numbers
thirties 58
this 7, 19, **31–43**
  as intensifier 41, 114
  difference between **this** and **that** 35–41
  in stories 41
  on the telephone 33
  referring to person 33
  with **kind** and **sort** 43
  in this way 40
  this and that 42
  see also Demonstratives
those 7, 19
  non-demonstrative uses 33–34
  all those 82
  those few 134
  those of 33, 34
  those which/who 33–34
  see also Demonstratives, **that**
thousand 56, 143–44
three
  two or three 59
thrice 65
through 85–86
thy 23
Time
  expressed by number alone 58
  use of **half** in times 71
  use of **quarter** in times 68
  this and **that** in relation to 37–39
time
  all the time 85
  every time 92
  some time 76
  the whole time 88
  times in multipliers 65, 66
Time periods 61, 71, 76, 84–85, 91, 93, 133, 134, 144
to
  in expressions with **much** 111–12
  enough...to 145
  quarter to 68

185

tons (of) 122
too
　much too 111
　too few 133
　too many 112–13
　too much 112–13, 115
twelfth 63, see also Fractions, Ordinal numbers
twenties 58–59
twice 65–66
two
　in approximate numbers 59
Uncount nouns 6–7
us
　as demonstrative 19, 44
Verbs
　used with **little** and **a little** 130–31
　used with **much** 109–10, 111
very 113, 133
　at the very least 129
way
　all the way 85
　either way 140
　in this way 40
we
　as demonstrative 19, 44
week 38, 96
what 6, 14, 16, 19, **150–51**
　as 'wh'-word determiner **45–49**, **51–52**
　difference between **what** and **which** 4, 47
　in exclamations 150–51
　in noun clauses 51–52
　in questions 49
　what a 150–51
　what few 134
　what is more 118
　what kind of 48
　what little 126
　what sort of 48
whatever 53–54

which 6, 19, **45–52**
　as quantifier 46
　as relative determiner 50
　difference between **which** and **what** 4, 47
　in noun clauses 51–52
　in questions 49
　in relative clauses 49–50
　referring to whole clause 50
　that which 34
　those which 33–34
　which one(s) 46–47
whichever 53
while
　every once in a while 91
who
　those who 33–34
whoever's 53–54
whole 88–89
whom 51
who's 48–49
whose 6, 19, **45–52**
　compared with possessive determiners 48
　in noun clauses 51–52
　in questions 49
　in relative clauses 49–51
'Wh'-word determiners **45–54**
with 85
world
　all the world 85
wrong 86
year 38, 76, 91, 96–97, 134
yon 37
yonder 37
you
　as demonstrative 16, 19, 44
　you are a one 62
your 19, 21
　see also Possessive determiners
yours 21, 22
　see also Possessive pronouns
Zero article 5